APPLE LVERS
COOK BOOK

by Shirley Munson and Jo Nelson

**GOLDEN
WEST** ☼
PUBLISHERS

Cover designs by Bruce R. Fischer/Book Studio
Cover photo by Linda F. Thomas

Acknowledgments

The authors wish to express their deep appreciation to Dr. Cecil Stushnoff, Colorado State University, formerly of the Department of Horticultural Science, University of Minnesota; to Dr. Leonard Hertz, Dr. Emily Hoover and Dr. James Luby, all of the Department of Horticultural Science, University of Minnesota; to Dr. H. W. Schafer, Department of Food Science and Nutrition, University of Minnesota; to Dr. Eugene Mielke, Agricultural Experiment Station, Hood River, Oregon; to Dr. Michael Kilby, Extension Fruit Specialist, University of Arizona; to Dr. Robert Lamb, New York State Agricultural Experiment Station; to Anna Peterson and Esther Peterson for their Apple Chutney recipe; to Mary (Hart) Sorensen, food writer of the *Star Tribune*, Minneapolis, Minnesota for her recipe, Em's Eggless Applesauce Fruit Cake, and for her helpful suggestions.

A special thanks goes to Christine Hipp Hlavacek for her valuable assistance in testing recipes and to Kathleen L. Lloyd for her secretarial assistance.

Library of Congress Cataloging-in-Publication Data

Munson, Shirley.
Apple-lovers' cook book / by Shirley Munson and Jo Nelson.

Includes index.
1. Cookery (Apples) I. Nelson, Jo II. Title.
TX813.A6M85 1989   641.6'411—dc20   89-23639
ISBN 0-914846-43-4   CIP

Printed in the United States of America

10th Printing © 2000

Golden West Publishers   **(602) 265-4392**
4113 N. Longview   **1-800-658-5830**
Phoenix, AZ 85014, USA   **FAX 602-279-6901**

Contents

Apples in America...5
How Well Do You Know Your Apple Varieties?...13
Know Your Apples (charts)...20
Tender Loving Care from Grower to You...25
Good to Eat and Good for You, Too!...29
Recipes:
  Appetizers...33
  Salads...35
  Main & Side Dishes...41
  Breads, Buns, Muffins & Rolls...45
  Bars and Cookies...53
  Cakes...59
  Pies...71
  Desserts...81
  Beverages...93
  Microwave...97
Preserving Apples...99
  Jelly & Preserves...101
  Applesauce...104
  Freezing & Drying...105
Fun with Apples...109
Index...113

Guide to Buying Apples

Buying apples by the bushel or half-bushel is usually more economical than buying smaller amounts. But before you buy a large quantity, ask yourself: How soon will I use these apples? Do I have the proper place to store them?

Your guide is to buy what you can store properly or use without waste. Medium-size apples—a little less than 3 inches in diameter—are usually the best buy.

Suppose you want enough apples so you can go on an apple pie baking binge, with enough fruit left over for the family's lunches and snacks. Here's a table to help you calculate how many apples you need or can use, whether you're buying by the bushel, by pounds, or by numbers of apples.

1 lb. apples = 2 large, 3 medium, or 4 to 5 small; or
approximately 3 cups peeled, sliced
or diced fruit.

2 lbs. apples = 6 to 8 medium-size;
or enough for 1 (9″) pie.

1 bu. apples = 40 lbs. or about 120 medium-size;
enough for about 20 (9″) pies,
or 16 to 20 quarts applesauce.

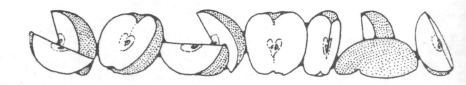

Apples in America

- Apples Come to America
- Apples a Mainstay in Early America
- Apples Prized for Cider
- Apple Butter and Apple Pies
- The First Apple Tree in Vancouver

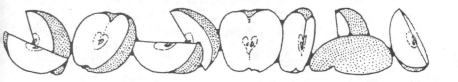

Apples in America

"The apple car is here! Hey, kids, hurry! The apple car just came!" Screams of delight filled the air as the news spread among children shuffling home from school. Suddenly boys and girls were alive with energy, sprinting toward the railroad tracks.

In the days when freight trains were commonplace in small towns of America, villagers looked forward to the crisp autumn day the "freight" would pull a boxcar loaded with apples to a siding. As the door was pushed open, throngs of children were waiting to catch the red apples tossed to them. From town and farm, people came with gunny sacks and bushel baskets to stock up on apples, always a good buy from the apple car. Stored in a cool, moist cellar, the apples would last most of the winter.

Often called "the king of fruits," the apple is probably the oldest fruit known to man. Many believe that apples were the forbidden fruit in the Garden of Eden. In the Old Testament, in Deuteronomy 32:10 and Psalms 17:8, both Moses and David used the expression, "the apple of his eye." Greek mythology tells of a golden apple inscribed "to the fairest" which actually caused the Trojan war.

Apple trees grew wild thousands of years ago in central and southwest Asia, China and the Near East. From there, the fruit was carried to Turkey, Israel and Europe. Charred remains of apples found in Stone Age lake dwellings in central Europe show that prehistoric man ate apples and dried them as well. When people began to cultivate crops, they planted seeds from wild apples in their gardens. At least 22 varieties were known to the Romans 2,000 years ago; when they invaded Britain, they brought along their apples.

In the Middle Ages, cultivation of apples (and other fruits) was taken over by the monasteries. The monks experimented with ways to make orchards more fruitful; their cultural methods became the foundation of apple orcharding.

Apples Come to America

By the time Columbus sailed west, apples were the most important cultivated fruit in Europe. The Spaniards who followed Columbus to the New World brought apples to Mexico and South America. The French carried them to the St. Lawrence River area in Canada. Years later, Spanish priests who founded missions in our Southwest planted apple seeds.

Crabapples were growing wild in North America but the fruits were bitter, sour and very small. In 1629, the Puritans of the Massachusetts Bay Colony planted apple seeds from England. The trees flourished in the cool climate, and from the time of the first settlements, apples have played an important role in American social history.

As the frontier moved westward, one man can be given more credit than any other for the hundreds of apple orchards that sprang up on the newly settled farms between the Allegheny and the Mississippi, and particularly in the Ohio River Valley: John Chapman—"Johnny Appleseed."

> "Remember Johnny Appleseed,
> All ye who love the apple;
> He served his kind by Word and Deed,
> In God's grand greenwood chapel."

—William Henry Venable, "Johnny Appleseed"

He has become a mythical figure, a hero of the folklore of the frontier, immortalized in song, story and poetry. The legendary picture is of a wiry man of medium height plodding along barefoot, wearing a coffee sack shirt, carrying a leather knapsack of apple seeds on his back. His saucepan hat doubled as a kettle in which to cook his mush.

The real John Chapman was born in 1774 in Leominster, Massachusetts, in September, appropriately—apple-picking time. Land records show that by the time he was 23—in expectation of a land rush to the area—he had selected a spot in beautiful virgin country in western Pennsylvania for his first apple planting. Until he died at the age of 71, he was obsessed with his passion for planting nurseries, moving them westward as the frontier was opening, always just ahead of the rush of settlers.

Every pioneer family hoped to have an orchard yielding fruit in as short a time as possible. As soon as they cleared some land and raised a cabin, an early task was to plant apple trees. An orchard was considered a sign of permanence as well as mastery of the land.

The problem at the time was to get trees. And that was where John Chapman—Johnny Appleseed—came in. He would visit the cider presses in the older, settled areas, wash out of the crushed apple pulp a bushel or two of seeds, pack them in his leather pouch and return to plant them on land he had bought or leased and cleared. After sowing the seeds, he would enclose the plot with a brush fence and spend some time cultivating his planting. Finally, he would put someone in charge to tend and later to sell his trees to new settlers. Then Johnny Appleseed would move on to another favorable spot with another pouch of seeds and go through the same operation.

Actually, there was nothing unusual about gathering seeds at cider presses and planting them in new clearings for future orchards. Many settlers did that. What was unusual about John Chapman was his larger plan of moving his apple seedling business westward with the frontier.

Forging into the wilderness, this Yankee tree peddler established a chain of plantings in western Pennsylvania, then across Ohio and into Indiana—always ahead of the big push of pioneers looking for good land. By the time settlers arrived, his seedling stock was ready to be sold or given away to those who could not afford to buy the trees.

Possibly his perseverance in establishing his trail of nurseries was connected with his missionary zeal for the Swedenborgian faith. As one of the earliest American converts to the Church of the New Jerusalem, it was his urgent desire to spread its doctrines. Besides his apple seeds, he carried with him as many of the publications of Emanuel Swedenborg as he could obtain. Whenever he could persuade anyone to read the books or tracts he carried, he would leave them until he came again. He would even divide the publications into parts, to make them go further, returning later with another section so they could be read in proper order. This unusual missionary actually started a kind of traveling library on the frontier!

Dressed in what looked like cast-off clothing, an animal skin or old hat on his head, his hair hanging down to his shoulders, usually barefooted, he was always the eccentric wanderer. He had no home of his own. He traveled back and forth on foot, horseback, by dugout or canoe to attend to his seedlings. He camped wherever he happened to be when night fell, or stopped at a cabin to ask for lodging. Usually he insisted on sleeping on the floor. He might read some of his Swedenborgian tracts to the elders or entertain the children with tales of his adventures in the wilderness with rattlesnakes, bears and wolves. He never carried a gun, for he had a deep respect for all living things. He died as he lived, looking after his plantings.

John Chapman's contribution in starting hundreds of apple orchards across the new frontier was probably not recognized by his peers in the early 1800's. But today, Johnny Appleseed is a hero. Bridges and highways have been named for him, while apple festivals and plaques erected by historical and horticultural societies keep alive the myths and facts about this itinerant nurseryman. He identified himself as "by occupation a gatherer and planter of apple seeds." He has become a patron saint of orcharding and conservation.

Apples a Mainstay in Early America

To the early American pioneers, apples were a basic crop. No other fruit could be so easily started, and none was more versatile. The best apples were eaten fresh for dessert and made into pies and sauces. For later use, some of the fruit was peeled, sliced and hung in strings to dry from the rafters, or dried in the sun.

The French surveyor-farmer-explorer, St. John de Crevecoeur, who settled on a farm in New York in late 1769, described how a great stage was erected outdoors on which apples were thinly spread to dry.

"They were soon covered with bees and wasps and sucking flies of the neighborhood," wrote Crevecoeur. "This accelerates the operation of drying. Now and then they are turned. At night they are covered with blankets. If it is likely to rain, they are gathered and brought into the house. This is repeated until they are perfectly dried...

"It is astonishing to what small size they shrink," he went on. "The method of using them is this. We put a small handful in warm water overnight; next morning they are swelled to their former size; and when cooked either in pies or dumplings, it is difficult to discover whether they are fresh or not."

Apples Prized for Cider

The least choice apples from those early orchards were hauled to a nearby cider press and made into cider and vinegar.

Cider was the staple beverage in most households in Colonial America—barrels of it for the family to drink in early autumn when it was sweet and delicious. The early settlers had brought with them from the Old World their taste for cider as well as the knowledge of how to make it.

In the 1720's a village of 40 families is said to have made 3,000 barrels of cider. "Cider was, next to water, the most abundant and the cheapest fluid to be had in New Hampshire, while I lived there," wrote Horace Greeley, "often selling for a dollar a barrel. In many a family of six or eight persons, a barrel tapped on Saturday barely lasted a full week..." Since milk was considered a hazard for drinking, cider was the national beverage at least through the first half of the nineteenth century.

The White House Cook Book, published in 1887, gave a variety of suggestions on how to keep cider. Among them was this recipe:

"To keep cider sweet, allow it to work until it has reached the state most desirable to the taste, and then add one and a half tumblers of grated horse-radish to each barrel, and shake up well. This arrests further fermentation. After remaining a few weeks, rack off and bung up closely in clean casks."

The early American housewife needed cider and vinegar as flavorings and preservatives for the winter store of pickles, preserves, apple butters and mincemeats.

Apples, cider and vinegar could all be used as barter, too, for supplies the family might need and even to pay education expenses for the children. A diary dated 1805 mentions payment of "one-half barrel of cider for Mary's schooling."

Frontiersmen enjoyed hard cider as a normal social drink, providing cheer at weddings and other community gatherings. Often men carried a jug of hard cider to the woods or fields to help ease the backbreaking labor of a long day. In the first years on the frontier, however, before apple trees were producing, corn whiskey was the only alcoholic drink that could be made locally to any large extent. But as apples became abundant, part of the apple juice produced was diverted to make the highly potent liquor called applejack—the American term for apple brandy—sometimes referred to as "the essence of lockjaw." The fermented apple juice contained from .5 percent to 8 percent alcohol.

The apple juice from modern cider mills, unless sold to a distiller to make brandy, is usually pasteurized or treated with preservatives to keep it from fermenting. The sweet cider you buy in the grocery store or at a fruit stand is really apple juice, not cider. Fermented apple juice is hard cider.

Apple Butter and Apple Pies

The Pennsylvania Dutch can take credit for introducing apple butter to the American cuisine. Women of the neighborhood got together to chat and exchange gossip at apple paring bees. The apples they prepared were stirred into boiling cider in huge outdoor kettles. When it cooked down, it was a rich, dark, thick spread spiced with cloves, cinnamon or sassafras. Relished by every family, it was often eaten with cottage cheese *(schmierkase)* on slices of homemade bread. The Pennsylvania Dutch were also experts at drying apple slices, which they called *schnitz*, from the German word meaning "cut." The apples they dried in the oven or in the sun were used in pies and such other favorite dishes as *schnitz und knepp*, apples with dumplings.

A classic breakfast in Pennsylvania Dutch country consisted of fried apples, fried mush and sausages. For frying, they chose the tastiest apples from their orchards, and sprinkled them lightly with sugar and cinnamon before serving.

.Apple pie had been popular in Britain; in New England it soon became not only the standard dessert, but often a breakfast staple in many homes. Served with cheese, of course. "Apple pie without cheese is like a kiss without a squeeze," the saying went. At Yale College, every supper served for more than a hundred years is said to have included apple pie.

As the frontier moved westward, pioneer women carried with them the know-how for making apple pie. For many of the immigrants, however, apple pie was a strange but appealing new dessert. In 1851 a Norwegian immigrant who had settled in Wisconsin wrote home describing a wonderful dish called *Pai*, made of berries combined with sugar and syrup. "I can tell you this is something that glides easily down your throat; they also make the same sort of *Pai* out of apples...with syrup added, and that is really the most superb."

The Reverend Henry Ward Beecher, famous nineteenth century clergyman, paid an eloquent tribute to apple pie, declaring it should be anointed with sugar, butter and spices to form a "glorious unity...the morsels of apple neither dissolved nor yet in original substance, but hanging as it were in a trance between the spirit and the flesh of applehood..."

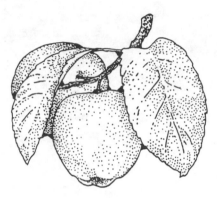

The First Apple Tree in Vancouver

Apples reached the Pacific Northwest in the early nineteenth century, not across the plains and mountains, but by sea. At a banquet in London in the winter of 1826, friends gave the captain of a Hudson's Bay Company vessel some seeds of a "good luck" apple. Captain Simpson was about to set sail on the hazardous voyage around Cape Horn to the Pacific Northwest; his friends wanted him and his men to have a reminder of their native England when they reached the new land. The good luck held; and, as his friends wished, Simpson planted the seeds in the spring of 1827, in the frontier outpost, Fort Vancouver, Washington.

From that beginning, the Washington apple industry has grown to be first in the nation. And the state's first apple tree still stands in the busy city of Vancouver, bearing fruit each year!

Commercial plantings in Washington spread rapidly through the eastern and central part of the state after the first irrigation project was completed in 1889. In 1894, the first railroad car of fruit was shipped from Yakima. Now refrigerated railroad cars plus special refrigerated trailer trucks move Washington apples to all parts of the United States each year.

The states of California, Michigan, New York, Pennsylvania, Virginia and Washington account for the major part of the United States crop. Washington ranks at the top of states in apple production. In Canada, British Columbia, Ontario and Nova Scotia produce the most apples.

Over half of the apples grown in North America are sold as fresh fruit. The rest are canned commercially as applesauce and sliced apples, dried, frozen or made into sweet juice, cider and vinegar.

How Well Do You Know Your Apple Varieties?

- Delicious: America's Favorite Eating Apple

- Golden Delicious: Second in Popularity

- Other Apple Varieties from Seedlings

- Peter Gideon and the Wealthy Apple

- What Variety Should You Buy

- How to Judge Apple Quality

- How to Store Apples for Longer Keeping

- Know Your Apples (charts)

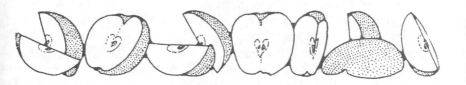

How Well Do You Know Your Apple Varieties?

Apples belong to the rose family. Have you ever noticed how apple blossoms resemble tiny wild roses?

At one time there were thousands of different apple varieties grown in this country, but most of these have now disappeared. Some succumbed to disease and insects, others were left to die out because they did not sell or store well. Some trees were cut down by temperance workers fighting the evils of cider and applejack. Of the varieties that still exist, only about 25 are grown extensively in the United States and Canada. Less than that number make up over 90 percent of all apples grown commercially, though there are many small plantings of other kinds. Some of the old varieties are now grown for their historical value in an experimental orchard established by the Worcester County Historical Society in Northgrafton, Massachusetts and in other specialty nurseries.

The wild apple, ancestor of our modern cultivated varieties, was small and often sour. Through the years, man selected the best fruit for eating from wild trees and used the seed from the better fruit for planting. In this way, the quality of apples gradually improved over the centuries.

Apples, however, are among the fruits whose seeds do not "breed true." New trees grown from seeds almost never produce fruit exactly like that of the parent. Hence most seedlings are worthless. But every so often one bears such superior fruit—better than that of its parent—that it is propagated as a new vartiety. In fact, many of the present important varieties originated as choice seedlings.

Trees for today's orchards are produced by budding or grafting. That means uniting parts of two plants so they grow as one. A *bud* or *scion*—a short piece of twig—from a superior tree is inserted into a young seedling tree. The scion forms the top of the new tree. The new tree will produce fruit exactly like that of the parent tree from which the scion or bud was taken. Today, instead of doing their own grafting or budding, growers usually buy trees from nurseries.

By budding or grafting onto certain kinds of stock, nurserymen can produce dwarf apple trees. They've become popular because they are easier to care for and easier to harvest. And they often start bearing fruit sooner than larger trees.

The art of grafting is very old; no one knows who first grafted a tree. Perhaps people developed the idea from seeing natural grafts in the woods, where a branch of one tree becomes wedged in the crotch of another. At any rate, by 800 B.C., the Greeks had already written about their grafting techniques. Johnny Appleseed, however, our itinerant pioneer nurseryman, stubbornly stuck to planting from seed, possibly because he was convinced that was what the good Lord intended.

Many of the land-grant colleges and universities in the United States have fruit breeding projects at experiment stations. They work to develop apples and other fruits especially adapted to the climate of that region. Thus scientific breeding has resulted in some fine apple varieties.

Delicious: America's favorite eating apple

The leading apple variety in the United States is Delicious. It's sometimes called Red Delicious to distinguish it from Golden Delicious, which holds the second place ranking in production.

The Delicious apple originated on the farm of Jesse Hiatt in Peru, Iowa, in the last half of the nineteenth century. The story goes that Mr. Hiatt had planted an apple tree named Bellflower. It did not live, but the seedling root sent up a sprout which he nursed into bearing in 1872.

Twenty-two years later, in 1894, the Stark Brothers Nursery in Louisiana, Missouri, invited exhibits of fruit from all over the world to their fruit fair. Intrigued by the offer of prizes for the best specimens of known and unknown varieties, Jesse Hiatt packed a barrel of apples from his tree and shipped it to the fair. When the president of the company, C. M. Stark, tasted one of the apples, he exclaimed, "My, that's delicious!" The apples won first prize, but Hiatt's name was lost in the handling.

Stark Brothers repeated the fair the following year and again Hiatt sent a barrel of apples. This time the tag bearing his name was not lost. Sensing that this apple would win consumer approval, the Starks purchased all rights from Jesse Hiatt to propagate it as a new variety. The following year they introduced the new apple into commercial production.

There are more Red Delicious apples sold in the United States than any other variety, most of them grown in Washington state. Washington has more than 2½ million Delicious trees.

The fruit of America's favorite eating apple can easily be recognized by its elongated shape, the five distinct knobs at the blossom end, its sweet flavor and aroma. It has been dubbed "the sheep nose apple" because some see a resemblance between the knobby end and the nose of a sheep.

Golden Delicious: second in popularity

Golden Delicious is the product of a chance seedling discovered on the Anderson Mullens farm in Clay County, West Virginia. It was probably the result of a cross between Grimes Golden and the Golden Reinette, also known as English Pippin. In 1914, Mullens sent some of the fruit, which he called Mullens' Yellow Seedling, to Stark Brothers Nursery. The nursery was looking for a variety to complement its Red Delicious apple and purchased the new seedling, naming the fruit Golden Delicious.

Because of their thin skins, Golden Delicious apples were often bruised by the time they reached markets after shipping. But improved methods of packing, new containers and special handling procedures have now eliminated most of the problems.

Other apple varieties from seedlings

The third most important apple variety in the United States—and the leading variety in Canada—is McIntosh, descended from a chance seedling found in 1796 on a pioneer farm in Ontario, Canada. The apple was named for John McIntosh, the farmer who transplanted the clump of young apple trees he discovered while clearing land. By 1830 only one of the transplanted trees had survived, but the family liked the fruit from it so well that McIntosh's son Allen propagated it for his nursery business by budding and grafting. The original tree bore fruit for more than a hundred years.

By 1900 the variety was well known throughout the Northeast. Today, McIntosh is the favorite apple in New England and New York state. However, Empire, with characteristics of both McIntosh and Red Delicious, is fast climbing in popularity.

Other choice varieties that came from seedlings include Baldwin, discovered by a surveyor working near Lowell, Massachusetts, in the 1790's'; Northern Spy, found in Bloomfield, New York, about 1800; and Wealthy, developed from a seedling in Minnesota.

Peter Gideon and the Wealthy apple

The experience of Peter Gideon in developing the Wealthy apple in Minnesota is an example of the discouragement, yet courageous persistence of some of the early fruit breeders. In 1853, Gideon had moved with his family from Clinton, Illinois, to Minnesota and in 1858, he took up a claim of 160 acres of land on Lake Minnetonka, near Minneapolis.

For 41 years he worked to develop fruits for Minnesota growers that could survive the rigorous climate. In his first experiments after coming to Minnesota, he planted 30 varieties of apple trees and other fruits, to which he added annually. At the end of 10 years, rugged Minnesota winters had killed all of them except one lone seedling of a Siberian crab.

Though discouraged, impoverished, and with a large family to support, Gideon was still determined to produce a high quality apple hardy in the northern United States. He used his last $8 to send to Maine for seeds and scions. Eventually his dogged tenaciousness paid off; by 1868 he had successfully developed the Wealthy apple from the seed of the Siberian crabapple. He named it for his wife, Wealth.

In 1912 a tablet in memory of Peter Gideon was erected on land that was once his farmstead, where he grew the original Wealthy apple.

What Variety Should You Buy

Some apple varieties are best for eating fresh, others for pie, still others for sauce or for baking. Some of the varieties you particularly like may not be available in retail stores. Depending on where you live, you may be able to obtain them at orchard sales rooms or apple barns. One of the joys of autumn is to take your family for a ride into the country to an apple orchard, an apple barn or a roadside stand. At many orchards, now, you can have the fun of picking your own apples.

Your family probably has definite likes when it comes to choosing an apple variety for eating fresh. While many apples are all purpose, some varieties are better than others for pies, sauce and baking. The chart "Know Your Apples" describes characteristics of the most commonly available apples that come onto the market in mid and late fall. You'll want to refer to it as a guide for trying new varieties—and to get full satisfaction from the apples you buy.

What about early apples? Almost all of the apples that mature in late summer and early fall are local varieties. They're not shipped to market; they don't store well. Mostly, they're your "backyard apples," or available locally in season at roadside stands.

Depending on where you live, you may recognize their names: Beacon (also called Early Delicious, Fenton, Miller Red), Crimson Beauty, Duchess (or Oldenburg), Early McIntosh (Rob Roy), Gravenstein, Lodi, Mantet, Melba, Oriole, Paula Red, Summer Champion, Summer Red, Tydeman's Red, Wealthy, Wellington, William's Red and Yellow Transparent.

The most widely grown of these early apples are Duchess, Wealthy and recently Paula Red. Duchess is too tart for fresh eating, but good for pies, sauce and freezing. Wealthy is an all-purpose apple, medium-tart. Paula Red, usually red, is crisp, juicy and slightly tart.

Most of the early apples are best for fresh eating, salads, fruit cups and desserts. They are also suitable for pie and sauce, and for canning and freezing. Refrigerate them and use them (or preserve them) within 3 to 4 weeks—they do not store well.

How to Judge Apple Quality

Here are the quality indicators to look for when you buy fresh apples:
- Bright, sparkling color for the variety you select. Good color indicates full flavor. Don't be turned off by russeting—rough reddish-brown skin on part of the apple; this will not affect eating quality or flavor.
- Firmness, which is also a sign of good condition. Apples should be reasonably free of bruises since they may indicate poor handling, overripeness or even the beginning of decay. But when you test firmness, don't pinch—or you'll be responsible for adding bruises.
- The U.S. grade label, another indication of quality. Always check grade label before you buy. The federal government has specified grade standards based on maturity, degree of ripeness, uniformity of size, color and absence of blemishes. Most states have either adopted these grade standards or have similar ones. U.S. Extra fancy and U.S. Fancy are the top grades. U.S. No. 1 meets minimum grade standards.

If you should buy apples in perforated polyethylene bags, you should find this information on the packaging: variety, weight, size of apple, U.S. grade. For example, if you were buying Jonathan apples, you might find printed on the bag: Jonathan apples, U.S. Fancy, 2½″ minimum, net wt. 48 oz. (3 lb.), washed.

How to Store Apples for Longer Keeping

If you buy apples in a perforated polyethylene bag, keep them in that bag in the refrigerator. The perforations allow air to enter the bag so that apples—with their living cells—can breathe. If you buy them in bulk, store them in the hydrator or in a covered container in the refrigerator to maintain proper humidity.

Apples purchased by the bushel or half-bushel will keep best, of course, in a cool, humid cellar. Unfortunately, modern homes rarely have cool cellars. You're in luck, though, if you have a second refrigerator—perhaps in the basement—where you have room for them. The refrigerator is an ideal place to keep apples over a long period, provided they are in a well covered container; otherwise they will dry out very quickly. With no refrigerator space available, keep apples in as cool a place as possible and line the bushel basket (or box) with aluminum foil or polyethylene to help prevent moisture loss. To increase humidity, you might also place a small container of water among the apples or cover the basket or box with moist towels.

Regardless of the quantity of apples you buy, a cardinal rule is to handle them gently to avoid bruising.

Red apples, polished to a high gloss, make a handsome centerpiece. But don't keep apples in the fruit bowl for days at a time. Apples will soften as much in a day at room temperature as they will in 10 days at 32° F. Moreover, the dry air will draw moisture and the fruit will shrivel, lose flavor and develop tough skin. So, to keep apples crisp and of good eating quality, hustle them back into the refrigerator between the times you need a decorative bowl of fruit for a centerpiece or snacking.

Not too many years ago, once winter was over, it was hard to find good, firm apples to buy. But greatly improved varieties which keep longer and modern technology have solved that problem. Now you'll have little trouble getting good apples the year round. Fruit to be held for winter or spring selling is put into refrigerated storage immediately after it is harvested. It is cooled rapidly to about 32° F. where it is held until it is marketed.

Apples keep even better in controlled (CA) or modified (MA) atmosphere storage. This controlled or modified atmosphere slows the life processes of the fruit cells and helps keep the fruit from getting soft.

Thus we have improved varieties and refrigerated and controlled atmosphere storage to thank for stretching the apple season so we can keep munching crisp apples until green apple time comes around once more.

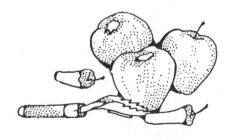

Know Your Apples

MID-FALL Variety	Characteristics	Uses	Availability in U.S. and Canada
Cortland	Medium size, attractive red with white flesh, similar to McIntosh. Holds fresh color well in salad. Mild flavor.	Salad, sauce, pie, baking, fresh eating and freezing.	East, Central
Delicious (Red)	Medium size, striped to solid red. Rich, sweet and mellow. Distinguished by elongated shape and five knobs at blossom end.	A favorite for fresh eating and salads. Not recommended for pie or cooking.	West, East, Central, South. Most available of all apple varieties and most popular in U.S. Washington State is number one producer.
Empire	Medium size, red-on-yellow to all red. Crisp and juicy.	Excellent for fresh eating. Good for salad, sauce and pie.	East, Central
Fuji	Small, sweet, crisp, juicy, low acid.	Fresh eating, salad, sauce.	West, also Japan.
Gala	Dull red, blushed or striped, yellow undercast. Sweet, crisp, juicy.	Fresh eating, salad.	West also New Zealand, South America and Southern Europe.
Golden Delicious	Medium size, attractive yellow. Flavor rich, tangy, sweet. Similar in texture and shape to Red Delicious.	Fresh eating, salad, baking. Excellent all-purpose apple.	West, East, Central, South. Second most popular variety in U.S.

MID-FALL Variety	Characteristics	Uses	Availability in U.S. and Canada
Grimes Golden	Mild and sweet. Green-yellow to golden yellow.	Excellent for fresh eating, salad. Good cooking apple.	East, Central
Haralson	Medium size, attractive red, tart and juicy.	All-purpose: pie, sauce, fresh eating, baking, freezing. A favorite for caramel apples.	Central.
Idared	Attractive solid red, mild, crisp, small core.	Fresh eating, sauce, pie, freezing.	West, East, Central.
Jonathan	Below medium size, solid bright red. Tart, tender, juicy. Sweet flavor when cooked.	All-purpose: fresh eating, salad, pie, sauce, freezing.	West, East, Central, South. Usually off the market by December.
McIntosh	Medium size, nearly solid bright red. Rich flavor. High quality for eating, but soft when cooked.	Fresh eating, sauce, pie, baking, freezing.	East, Central, West, South. Leading variety in Canada and third most important variety in U.S.
Northwestern Greening	Attractive green or yellow, large size, slightly tart.	Pie, sauce, freezing.	East, Central
Rhode Island Greening	Small to medium size, green to yellow-green, mildly acid.	Sauce, pie.	East, Central.
Spartan	McIntosh type. Firm flesh, crisp, juicy, mildly tart.	Fresh eating, salad, pie.	East, Central, West.

LATE FALL Variety	Characteristics	Uses	Availability in U.S. and Canada
Baldwin	Dull red, mild flavor, firm texture.	Fresh eating, pie, sauce	East
Connell Red	Solid bright red, medium to large size, sweet, juicy.	Fresh eating, salad, baking.	Central, East.
Fireside	Large size, attractive, red, sweet.	Fresh eating, salad, baking.	Central
Granny Smith	Large, green skin, crisp, juicy, tart.	Fresh eating, salad, sauce, pie.	West, also New Zealand, Australia, Southern Europe, South America.
Jonagold	Large size, yellow-gold, red blush, juicy, crisp.	Excellent fresh eating and salad. Good sauce, baking, pie, freezing.	West, East rapidly growing popularity in Europe.
Mutsu (Crispin- English name)	Medium to large, yellow-green, juicy, sub-acid, crisp.	Fresh eating, salad, sauce and pie.	East, also Japan.
Northern Spy	Large, striped red, tender, crisp and juicy with spicy flavor.	Fresh eating, pie, sauce, baking, salad.	East, Central
Rome Beauty	Red with red stripes, shallow cup around stem. Firm, medium-tart to sweet.	Best for baking and cooking, also for salad. Holds its shape in baking.	East, West, South, Central

LATE FALL Variety	Characteristics	Uses	Availability in U.S. and Canada
Stayman	Deep purplish-red, sometimes russeted. Rich flavor, moderately juicy.	Fresh eating, salad, pie, sauce, baking.	East, South
Winesap	Deep, purplish red, winelike flavor, tangy, firm, crisp, very juicy.	Fresh eating, salad, pie, sauce, baking.	West, East, Central, South.
Yellow Newton	Greenish-gold, delicately tart, firm, crisp, juicy. Good keeping apple.	Fresh eating, pie, sauce, baking.	West
York Imperial	Green, lopsided shape, mildly tart, firm, excellent texture, creamy yellow color when cooked.	Sauce, baking, pie, fresh eating, salad.	South, East. Limited fresh distribution because of demand for commercial processing.

CRABAPPLES* Variety	Characteristics	Uses	Season
Centennial	Large, red-striped, yellow flesh, crisp, tender, juicy.	Fresh eating, sauce.	Late summer, early fall.
Chestnut	Large, crisp, juicy, spicy flavor. Keeps about 2 months.	Pickles, sauce, fresh eating.	Early to late fall.
Dolgo	Oval, solid bright red. Fruit a little small for pickles.	Jelly, pickles. Best crab for sparkling red jelly.	Late summer.
Whitney	Large, red-striped, juicy. Tender flesh becomes mealy.	Pickles, fresh eating, sauce.	Late summer.

*Availability of crabapples is limited to where they grow—in northern United States (primarily northern Great Plains) and Canada.

Tender Loving Care from Grower to You

- If Apples Weren't Sprayed

- Intensive Work Before Harvest

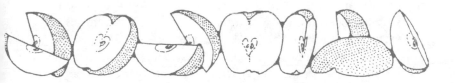

Tender Loving Care from Grower to You

You never need to worry about getting a wormy apple when you bite into one you've bought at your local market, orchard or roadside stand.

It's not by chance that these apples are a feast for the eye as well as the palate. Apple growing is no longer hit or miss, as it was on the frontier when the fruit was likely to be lopsided, often wormy and frequently very sour. Apple growing has become a science, called pomology. Although apples have been cultivated for thousands of years, horticulturists say that greater improvements have been made in the last 50 years than in all previous history because of modern technology.

Yet one of those advances in technology has come under attack by many Americans: the spraying with chemicals to combat insects and diseases which are among the worst enemies of the apple grower.

If Apples Weren't Sprayed

What would happen if apples in commercial orchards were not sprayed? Wormy apples, of course! Another result could be greatly reduced crops with consequent higher prices for the consumer.

Spraying has become a precise science. Since insect pests and diseases attack apples at different stages in development of the fruit, the grower must know exactly when to spray and with what. Different types of sprays are necessary for other purposes, too—such as the stop-drop sprays to prevent apples from dropping just before harvest and causing huge losses. The correct materials must be applied at precisely the right time. In commercial orchards, this is too big a job to be done by hand, so the grower must use powerful machines to cover the trees thoroughly with the protective mist.

But how can you be sure that the pesticide won't harm the food you eat? The answer is that federal agencies keep a vigilant eye on their use. The chemicals are tested in the laboratory and in the field for safe use. Tolerances have been set—standards for the safe level of chemical residue that may remain on the fruit when harvested. This is an almost infinitesimal amount, usually stated as parts per million. You, yourself, can take further precautions by washing apples before eating them.

Many other jobs are necessary to produce those beautiful apples for you. Once the orchard is planted the trees must be pruned in late winter each year to give the fruit better color and size, and to make spraying and harvesting easier. Then the trees must be fertilized so they will bear well, and they must be pollinated.

When the apple trees burst into bloom and the orchard is a pink and white fairyland, the grower brings in hives of honey bees to speed pollination. The reason: to insure a crop of well developed apples.

Essentially all commercial apple varieties are unable to produce fruit from their own pollen. To provide necessary cross-pollination, a grower may plant one Golden Delicious or Jonathan tree among ten Red Delicious trees. If the bees don't do their job of pollination satisfactorily, you might get a lopsided apple!

Intensive Work Before Harvest

Cultivation, irrigation (in some areas) and spraying when necessary follow blossomtime. Early in the growing period the orchardist must thin out half or two-thirds of the tiny green apples if the bloom has been heavy. Thinning is one of the most vital jobs if the grower is to harvest a crop of large, well formed, richly colored apples. Also, with thinning, food reserves will be conserved to produce fruit buds for next year's crop.

Although machines are used for many purposes in the orchard, most of the fruit is harvested by hand by skilled pickers. Again, proper timing is crucial. Once apples are harvested, people and machines work together to do the washing, sorting and grading of the fruit, packing and storing before market.

Thus the top quality fruit you enjoy today is the result of a large capital investment along with intensive work in planting, cultivating, pruning, pollinating, controlling insects and diseases, thinning and harvesting, storing, packing and marketing. The grower needs patience, too—the patience to wait at least four or five years for young trees to come into bearing, and eight or nine years before the orchard can be considered profitable.

You can see that those perfectly shaped red and golden-yellow apples you buy are the products of thousands of hours of tender loving care by growers, so that you as a consumer can have the very best.

Good to Eat, and Good for You, Too!

Aroma and taste combine to make apples among the most appealing of fruits. Their spicy fragrance and delicious flavor whet your appetite.

But they have many other virtues. Their low calorie content makes them welcome in the diets of the weight-conscious. Depending on variety, a medium-size apple counts only 75 to 85 calories. Apples are a perfect snack food because their natural fruit sugars provide quick energy, while the bulky pulp gives you a filled-up feeling. Nor do individuals on low-sodium diets need to restrain themselves from eating apples; they contain very little sodium.

Apples are a source of small amounts of Vitamins A and C, thiamin, riboflavin, niacin, calcium, phosphorus, potassium and some copper, iron and manganese. However, the amount of Vitamin C (ascorbic acid) you get from an apple will vary, depending on when and how you eat it.

A large summer apple furnishes about 22 milligrams of Vitamin C if eaten whole, but only 14 milligrams if peeled. A fall or winter apple of the same large size has about 14 to 15 milligrams if you peel it. After storage, the amount of Vitamin C drops as much as half.

Apples help keep you regular. The pectin in apples combines with water to form non-irritating bulk which helps intestinal activity— digestion and elimination.

Apples are thirst-quenchers too: they're 85 percent water. Little wonder that backpackers and football fans tuck apples into their pockets, and brown-baggers include them in their lunches. One apple is said to have the thirst-slaking capability of a half a glass of water.

While many fruits can be obtained only seasonally in our markets, apples are available the year round. So it's quite possible for you to have that "apple a day" to "keep the doctor away." Of course, confirmed apple eaters will tell you they eat apples for the sheer enjoyment of this flavorful, satisfying fruit. Perhaps that's the best argument there is for apples.

Recipes

- Apple Appetizers
- Apple Salads
- Main Dishes and Side Dishes
- Breads, Buns, Muffins and Rolls
- Bars and Cookies
- Apple Cakes
- Apple Pies
- Apple Desserts
- Apple Beverages
- Microwave Recipes

Recipe Notes

Apple Appetizers

Apple Dip

8 oz. CREAM CHEESE
½ cup SALAD DRESSING
½ cup shredded CHEDDAR
   CHEESE

½ cup chopped APPLES
APPLE SLICES (cored
   but not peeled)

Combine all ingredients. Refrigerate. Serve with apple slices or crackers. Makes about two cups.

Creamy Apple Dip

8 oz. CREAM CHEESE
¼ cup BROWN SUGAR
¼ cup POWDERED SUGAR
1 tsp. VANILLA

2 tsp. MILK
APPLE SLICES (cored
   but not peeled)

Beat cream cheese until smooth. Add sugars and vanilla. Beat until creamy. Add milk gradually until mixture is dipping consistency. Serve with apple slices. Makes about two cups.

- *Memo to meal planner: Use a variety of firm red, green and golden apples. Dip apple slices in a lemon juice solution (one tablespoon lemon juice to one quart water) or sprinkle apple slices with pure lemon juice and toss (or use a fruit preservative following label directions). Drain and arrange on platter with dip.*

Apple Spread

1 pkg. (8-oz.) CREAM CHEESE
1 Tbsp. MILK
1 cup finely chopped RED
   APPLES (not peeled)

½ cup pitted, chopped DATES
½ cup finely chopped PECANS
APPLE SLICES (cored
   but not peeled)

Beat cream cheese and milk. Stir in apples, dates and nuts. Spread on slices of apple or crackers. Makes about two cups.

Cheddar Dip

8 oz. sharp CHEDDAR CHEESE
1/3 cup HALF AND HALF
½ tsp. prepared MUSTARD

APPLE SLICES (cored but not peeled)

Allow wrapped cheese to come to room temperature. Remove wrap and cut cheese in cubes. Add half and half and mustard. Beat with electric mixer or blender until almost smooth. Makes about 1¼ cups.

Cut unpeeled apples into slices and arrange around bowl of dip.

Apple Appetizers

Core an unpeeled apple and slice it into rings. On a large plate arrange the apple rings on which you have spread any of the following:

- Cream cheese, softened with orange juice, mixed with raisins and finely-chopped nuts
- Cream cheese and apple butter
- Cream cheese with finely-chopped dates and nuts
- Peanut butter and raisins
- Peanut butter and finely-chopped dates and nuts

Apple Appetizers for a Cookout

If you're roasting marshmallows by a campfire, try a roasted marshmallow on an apple slice, top it with a piece of a chocolate bar and then another slice of apple.

Or spread an apple slice with peanut butter, top with a roasted marshmallow and then another slice of apple.

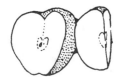

Apple Salads

Waldorf Salad

Oscar, maitre d' at the Waldorf-Astoria Hotel, created the Waldorf Salad of equal parts of raw apples and celery, moistened with mayonnaise, served on lettuce leaves. Later, someone added nuts to his creation.

2 cups unpeeled,
   diced APPLES
½ tsp. LEMON JUICE
⅛ tsp. SALT

1 cup chopped CELERY
½ cup chopped WALNUTS
¼ cup MAYONNAISE
SALAD GREENS

Combine apples, lemon juice, salt, celery and walnuts. Fold in mayonnaise. Chill. Serve on salad greens. Makes six servings.

Tuna Apple Salad

1 can (12-oz.) TUNA,
   drained and flaked
1½ cups unpeeled, diced
   APPLES
½ cup CELERY

½ cup chopped WALNUTS
MAYONNAISE (or salad
   dressing)
LETTUCE

Combine tuna, apples, celery and walnuts. Add enough mayonnaise to moisten. Chill. Serve in lettuce cups. Makes four to six servings.

Golden Salad

2 cups shredded CARROTS
1 cup unpeeled, diced
   APPLES

½ cup RAISINS
1 tsp. LEMON JUICE
SALAD DRESSING

Combine carrots, apples, raisins and lemon juice. Add enough salad dressing to moisten. Chill. Makes four to five servings.

Festive Red and White Salad

½ cup RED CINNAMON
  CANDIES
1 pkg. (3-oz.) LEMON GELATIN
1 cup boiling WATER
1½ cups sweetened
  APPLESAUCE

1 pkg. (8-oz.) CREAM CHEESE,
  softened
½ cup chopped NUTS
½ cup chopped CELERY
½ cup MAYONNAISE

Dissolve cinnamon candies and gelatin in boiling water. Add applesauce; mix well. Pour half of mixture in 8" square baking pan. Chill until firm. Let remaining gelatin mixture stand at room temperature.

Stir cream cheese until smooth. Add nuts and celery; mix well. Stir in mayonnaise. Spread over chilled gelatin layer. Pour remaining gelatin mixture evenly on top. Chill until firm. Cut in squares. Makes six servings.

- *Memo to meal planner: This delicious salad is a perfect accompaniment to poultry and ham. To fill a 5½-cup star mold, multiply the ingredients in the gelatin-applesauce mixture by 1½ but use only one recipe of the cream cheese filling. Instead of making a layer of the cheese mixture, use it on top of the mold for an eye-catching salad.*

Waldorf Oriental

3 red APPLES, unpeeled,
  cored and chopped
1 Tbsp. LEMON JUICE
1 can (11-oz.) MANDARIN
  ORANGES, drained
  (reserve syrup)

½ cup MAYONNAISE
1 cup CELERY, cut diagonally
½ cup WALNUTS, chopped
FRESH GREENS
¼ cup ALFALFA SPROUTS
  (optional)

Sprinkle chopped apple with lemon juice and toss. Drain oranges. Combine two tablespoons syrup with mayonnaise. Add oranges, celery and walnuts to apples. Toss. Add mayonnaise mixture and toss until well-coated. Serve on fresh greens and garnish with alfalfa sprouts. Serves six.

Coleslaw Apple Salad

2 cups unpeeled, sliced
RED APPLES
½ cup golden RAISINS

6 cups prepared COLESLAW

Toss apples and raisins with coleslaw. Serves 8-10.

• *Memo to meal planner: Dip apple slices in lemon juice or fruit preservative mixture to prevent them from browning. Or use Cortland apples which do not brown easily.*

Blushing Apple Fruit Salad

2 cups whole CRANBERRIES
1/3 cup SUGAR
2 cups peeled, diced APPLES
½ cup canned CRUSHED
PINEAPPLE, drained

½ cup MINIATURE
MARSHMALLOWS
½ cup HEAVY CREAM,
whipped

Put cranberries through food grinder. Sprinkle with sugar. Let stand two hours. Drain.

Combine drained cranberries, apples, pineapple and marshmallows. Chill. Just before serving, fold in whipped cream. Makes six to eight servings.

Cinnamon Apple Salad

½ cup RED CINNAMON
CANDIES
½ cup SUGAR
2 cups WATER

6 medium APPLES
pared and cored
COTTAGE CHEESE

Combine cinnamon candies, sugar and water in 2-qt. saucepan. Bring to a boil, stirring constantly. Add apples and simmer, turning occasionally until tender. Remove apples; place in glass dish. Continue cooking sugar mixture until thick and syrupy. Remove from heat and pour over apples. Chill. Stuff cavity of apples with cottage cheese. Serve on lettuce. Makes six servings.

Chicken Salad with Apples and Curry Dressing

6 cups cut-up cooked CHICKEN
(preferably skinless chicken
breast—about 2 lbs.)
1½ cups diced CELERY
2 cups RED APPLES,
unpeeled, cored and diced
1½ cups seedless GRAPES
(green and red, halved)

1 cup PINEAPPLE TIDBITS
(canned in own juice,
drained)
1 cup slivered ALMONDS
(reserving some for garnish)
GREENS

Cut cooked chicken in bite-size pieces. Combine with celery, apples, grapes, nuts and pineapple. Fold in curry dressing. Serve on salad greens. Garnish with a few almonds. Serves five to six.

- *Memo to meal planner: Two pounds of boned, skinless chicken breasts will yield approximately six cups of cooked, cut-up chicken.*

Curry Dressing

2/3 cup MAYONNAISE
2/3 cup YOGURT
(or sour cream)

¼ cup APPLE JUICE
½ to 1 tsp. CURRY POWDER
(according to taste)

Blend all ingredients together. Fold gently into chicken mixture.

- *Memo to meal planner: A few slices of cantaloupe served to the side of the salad add color and flavor.*

Apple Cheese Salad

2 cups unpeeled, diced
APPLES
1 cup sliced CELERY
¾ cup canned PINEAPPLE
TIDBITS, drained

½ cup cubed CHEDDAR
CHEESE
½ cup SALAD DRESSING
(or mayonnaise)
LETTUCE

Combine apples, celery, pineapple, cheese and salad dressing; toss well. Serve on lettuce. Makes four to six servings.

Lime Applesauce Mold

1 cup APPLESAUCE
plus ¼ cup WATER
1 pkg. (3-oz.) LIME GELATIN

1 tsp. grated ORANGE PEEL
1 small bottle 7-UP

Heat applesauce and water to boiling and add to lime gelatin. Stir in orange peel. Slowly pour in the carbonated beverage, mixing carefully. Pour into mold and chill until set. Serves four to six.

• **Memo to meal planner:** *Make a Rosy Applesauce Mold by substituting raspberry gelatin for the lime and omitting the orange peel. Serve the Rosy Applesauce Mold with a dressing made of sour cream, just enough maraschino cherry juice to give it the right consistency and a few cherries cut up fine.*

Fruited Cranberry-Apple Salad

1 pkg. (6-oz.) STRAWBERRY
GELATIN
½ cup boiling WATER
1 can (1-lb.) WHOLE
CRANBERRY SAUCE
1½ cups GINGERALE
1 cup NUTS, chopped

1 cup unpeeled APPLES,
chopped
1 can (8-oz.) CRUSHED
PINEAPPLE, drained
1 BANANA, diced
1 pkg. (3-oz.) CREAM CHEESE,
softened

Dissolve gelatin in boiling water. Add cranberry sauce and gingerale. Cool until the consistency of uncooked egg white. Then add nuts, apples, pineapple and banana. Pour into 9x9″ pan. Chill until firm; then top with the softened cream cheese. Makes six to nine servings.

Apple-Crab Meat Salad

1 can (6½-oz.) CRAB MEAT
¾ cup unpeeled, diced
  RED APPLES
¼ cup slivered, toasted
  ALMONDS

3 Tbsp. MAYONNAISE
3 Tbsp. dairy SOUR CREAM
SALAD GREENS

Flake crab meat. Combine with apples and almonds. Combine mayonnaise and sour cream, and add to crab mixture. Toss to mix. Serve on salad greens. Makes two to three servings.

- *Memo to meal planner: Shrimp or lobster may be substituted for the crab meat. Serve with hot rolls or hot muffins.*

Apple-Orange-Cranberry Salad

2 pkgs. (6-oz. each) ORANGE
  GELATIN
1 cup boiling WATER
2 cans (1-lb. each) JELLIED
  CRANBERRY SAUCE
¾ cup ORANGE JUICE
2 tsp. grated ORANGE
  RIND (optional)

1 cup peeled, chopped APPLE
½ cup chopped CELERY
SALAD GREENS
1 pt. creamed
  COTTAGE CHEESE
¼ cup toasted, slivered
  ALMONDS (optional)

Dissolve gelatin in boiling water. Mash cranberry sauce and add with the orange juice. Mix well. Cool until the consistency of uncooked egg white. Then stir in grated orange rind, chopped apple and celery. Pour into five-cup (1½-quart) ring mold. Chill until firm.

Unmold on crisp salad greens. Fill center of ring with the cottage cheese and top with almonds. Makes approximately eight servings.

Main Dishes & Side Dishes

Meatballs and Apple Sauerkraut

1½ lbs. GROUND MEAT
(pork, beef, veal or turkey)
½ tsp. SALT
¼ tsp. PEPPER
½ tsp. POULTRY SEASONING
1 cup dry BREAD CRUMBS
1/3 cup MILK

3 tart APPLES
1 qt. SAUERKRAUT
3 Tbsp. SUGAR
1 Tbsp. VINEGAR
1 Tbsp. CARAWAY SEED
(optional)
COOKING OIL

Gently combine meat, salt, pepper, poultry seasoning, bread crumbs and milk. Shape into meatballs. Heat cooking oil in a heavy skillet and cook meatballs until done. Keep hot .

Peel, core and slice apples. In a saucepan, combine apples with sauerkraut, sugar, vinegar and caraway seed. Bring to a boil and simmer 15 minutes. Put into a serving dish and top with meatballs. Serves six.

- *Memo to meal planner: Select a combination of three meats from pork, veal, beef, turkey, using ½ pound of each, making a total of 1½ pounds.*

Pork Chops and Apples

2 Tbsp. BUTTER (or margarine)
6 PORK CHOPS
4 APPLES, peeled, cored
and sliced

¼ cup BROWN SUGAR
½ tsp. CINNAMON

Brown pork chops on both sides. Place apple slices in greased baking dish. Combine brown sugar and cinnamon and sprinkle over apples. Add pork chops. Cover and bake in 325° oven for 1½ hours. Serves six.

Apple Butternut Bake

1 large BUTTERNUT SQUASH
   (2 to 3 lbs.)
¼ cup BUTTER (or margarine)
1 Tbsp. BROWN SUGAR
¼ tsp. SALT

Dash of PEPPER
½ cup SUGAR
1½ qts. TART APPLES
   peeled, cored and sliced

Bake squash until tender (about 30 min.). Scrape out pulp and mash until smooth. Stir in butter (or margarine), brown sugar, salt and pepper. Set aside.

Heat butter (or margarine) in skillet, add apples and ½ cup sugar, and simmer on low heat until barely tender. Spread apples in large flat casserole and spoon squash over them.

Topping:

3 cups CORNFLAKES,
   coarsely crushed
½ cup chopped PECANS

2 Tbsp. melted BUTTER
   (or margarine)
1 cup BROWN SUGAR

Mix topping ingredients together and spread over squash. Bake at 350° or until heated through and light brown.

- *Memo to meal planner: This is a wonderful vegetable dish to serve with pork roast.*

Sweet Potato Apple Casserole

4 medium SWEET POTATOES
3 medium tart APPLES
2 Tbsp. FLOUR
2 Tbsp. BROWN SUGAR

2 Tbsp. BUTTER (or margarine)
½ cup APPLE JUICE (or water)
4 strips BACON, cut in half

Peel sweet potatoes and cut into ¼-inch slices. Peel, core and slice apples. Combine flour and sugar and lightly dredge the sweet potatoes and apples. Butter a casserole and alternately layer apples and sweet potatoes. Dot with butter. Add apple juice. Arrange bacon over the top. Cover and bake at 350° for 35 minutes or until tender. Uncover and bake 5-10 minutes until bacon is crisp. Serves 4-5.

Puffy Apple Omelet

1 large APPLE (peeled, cored
  and thinly sliced)
1 Tbsp. BUTTER (or margarine)
2 Tbsp. granulated SUGAR

4 EGGS, separated
1 tsp. VANILLA
1 tsp. POWDERED SUGAR

Melt butter (or margarine) in small fry pan. Add sliced apples and sprinkle with one tablespoon sugar. Saute until tender.

Separate eggs. Beat egg yolks with the vanilla until frothy. Beat whites until soft peaks form; then add the remaining one tablespoon sugar and beat until the whites form stiff peaks. Gently fold whites into yolk mixture and pour into a well greased 9-9½" omelet pan. Bake in a pre-heated 325° oven on the middle rack for 20 minutes. Remove from the oven, place the apple filling on one side and fold. Sprinkle with the powdered sugar. Serves two to three.

Apple Stuffing

¼ cup MARGARINE
½ cup chopped CELERY
½ cup chopped ONION
3 Tbsp. chopped PARSLEY
2 qts. peeled, diced APPLES

¼ cup BROWN SUGAR
1 tsp. SALT
¼ tsp. PEPPER
¼ tsp. SAGE
2 cups dry BREAD CUBES

Cook onions, celery and parsley slowly in melted margarine. Add apples and brown sugar. Cover and cook slowly until apples are tender but firm. Add salt, pepper, sage and bread cubes. Toss lightly with a fork. Place in greased casserole and bake for 45 minutes at 350° Makes about eight servings..

• *Memo to meal planner: This is especially good with roast pork, goose or turkey.*

Recipe Notes

_____

_____

_____

_____

_____

_____

_____

_____

_____

_____

_____

_____

_____

_____

_____

_____

_____

_____

_____

_____

_____

_____

_____

Breads, Buns, Muffins & Rolls

Applesauce Pecan Rolls

1 pkg. (13¾-oz) ROLL MIX
2 Tbsp. SUGAR
6 Tbsp. BUTTER (or margarine)
1¾ cups APPLESAUCE
1/3 cup BROWN SUGAR,
 firmly packed
½ cup chopped PECANS
CINNAMON

Prepare roll mix according to directions on package, adding 2 tablespoons sugar. Cover; let rise until doubled in bulk. Meanwhile add 2 tablespoons butter (or margarine) to applesauce; cook 10 minutes to evaporate some of the liquid, stirring occasionally. Melt remaining 4 tablespoons butter (or margarine) in 9″ baking pan; add brown sugar; heat until dissolved.

Roll out dough to 17x9″ rectangle. Spread with cooled applesauce and sprinkle with pecans and cinnamon. Roll up jelly roll fashion. Cut in 1-inch slices. Arrange cut side up in pan on sugar mixture. Cover; let rise until doubled in bulk.

Bake in 400° oven for 20-25 minutes or until golden brown. Serve hot. Makes 16 rolls.

Apple-Raisin Bread

1/3 cup BUTTER (or margarine)
1 cup SUGAR
1 EGG
2 cups FLOUR
1 tsp. BAKING POWDER
½ tsp. SODA
½ tsp. SALT
1/3 cup FRUIT JUICE
¾ cup GOLDEN RAISINS
¼ cup chopped PECANS
1 cup peeled, finely chopped
 TART APPLES

Cream butter, sugar and egg. Sift together flour, baking powder, soda and salt. Add dry ingredients alternately with the fruit juice. Fold in raisins, pecans and apples. Transfer batter to a well greased 9x5x3″ loaf pan or two smaller pans. Bake 45 minutes in 350° oven. Test for doneness.

Apple Blueberry Bread

3 cups FLOUR
1 cup SUGAR
1 Tbsp. BAKING POWDER
1 tsp. SALT
½ tsp. ground NUTMEG
2 EGGS, beaten

1½ cups APPLESAUCE
¼ cup melted BUTTER
  (or margarine)
2 cups BLUEBERRIES
¼ cup FLOUR
1 cup peeled, chopped
  APPLES

Sift together 3 cups flour, sugar, baking powder, salt and nutmeg
Mix eggs, applesauce and melted butter (or margarine). Combine th
two mixtures. Toss blueberries with ¼ cup flour and fold into batte
with apples. Pour batter into two greased and floured 8½x4½x2½
inch loaf pans. Bake in 350° oven 55 minutes or until done. Cool fo
10 minutes; then remove from pans. Cool. Makes two loaves.

Apple Apricot Loaf

2/3 cup boiling WATER
½ cup finely diced dried
  APRICOTS
2 cups FLOUR
2½ tsp. BAKING POWDER
½ tsp. BAKING SODA
½ tsp. SALT
½ tsp. ALLSPICE

MILK
½ cup SHORTENING
¾ cup SUGAR
1 EGG
1½ cups peeled, finely diced
  APPLES
½ cup chopped WALNUTS

Pour boiling water over apricots; let stand. Sift together flour
baking powder, soda, salt and allspice. Drain apricots, saving liquid
pat apricots dry with paper towels. Add enough milk to apricot liqui
to make 2/3 cup.

Cream shortening; add sugar gradually while continuing to beat
Beat in egg. Add dry ingredients alternately with liquid. Combin
apples, apricots and walnuts; fold in. Spoon into well-greased 9x5x3
loaf pan.

Bake in 350° oven 50 minutes or until loaf tests done. Turn out o
pan. Cool. Loaf is easier to slice if it stands overnight. Makes one loa

Apple Pecan Kuchen

¾ cup SUGAR
¼ cup SHORTENING
1 EGG, slightly beaten
½ cup MILK
1½ cups FLOUR
2 tsp. BAKING POWDER
½ tsp. SALT
½ tsp. CINNAMON
⅛ tsp. ground NUTMEG
⅛ tsp. ground CLOVES

½ cup BROWN SUGAR,
  firmly packed
2 Tbsp. FLOUR
1 tsp. CINNAMON
2 Tbsp. melted BUTTER
  (or margarine)
2 cups peeled, sliced APPLES
3 Tbsp. BUTTER
4 Tbsp. HONEY
¾ cup chopped PECANS

Cream together sugar and shortening. Add egg and mix well. Stir in milk. Sift together flour, baking powder, salt, cinnamon, nutmeg and cloves. Stir into creamed mixture until smooth. Spread half of the batter in a greased 9" baking dish.

Mix together brown sugar, 2 tablespoons flour, 1 teaspoon cinnamon and 2 tablespoons melted butter. Sprinkle over batter; then arrange sliced apples over crumbs. Cover with remaining batter.

Mix together 3 tablespoons butter (or margarine), honey and pecans. Sprinkle over top layer.

Bake in 375° oven 30-35 minutes or until golden brown. Makes 9 servings.

Apple Cheese Sandwich Bread

½ cup SHORTENING
2/3 cup SUGAR
2 EGGS, well beaten
1 cup ground APPLE
  (include peel)
2 cups FLOUR

1 tsp. BAKING POWDER
1 tsp. BAKING SODA
½ tsp. SALT
½ cup grated mild CHEDDAR
  CHEESE
¼ cup chopped WALNUTS

Cream together shortening and sugar. Add eggs and apple.

Sift together flour, baking powder, soda and salt. Add to creamed mixture, blending well. Add cheese and nuts. Pour into well-greased and floured 9x5x3" loaf pan.

Bake in 350° oven 60-65 minutes. Cool for 10 minutes; then remove from pan. Cool well. Makes one loaf.

Apple Honey Buns

2 cups FLOUR
2 tsp. BAKING POWDER
½ tsp. SALT
½ cup BUTTER (or margarine)
1 EGG, beaten
MILK
2 Tbsp. melted BUTTER
(or margarine)
¼ cup thick APPLESAUCE

2 Tbsp. BROWN SUGAR,
firmly packed
¼ cup SUNFLOWER SEEDS
¼ cup RAISINS
1/3 cup BROWN SUGAR,
firmly packed
¼ cup HONEY
2 Tbsp. BUTTER (or margarine)

Sift flour, baking powder and salt together. Cut in ½ cup butter (or margarine). Add enough milk to egg to make 2/3 cup. Slowly add to flour mixture to form a soft dough. Knead dough ½ minute and roll to 14x10″ rectangle.

Mix together 2 tablespoons butter (or margarine), applesauce, 2 tablespoons brown sugar, sunflower seeds and raisins. Spread over dough. Roll dough from long side and cut into eight slices.

Combine 1/3 cup brown sugar, honey and 2 tablespoons butter (or margarine) and heat enough to dissolve sugar. Spoon 1 tablespoonful topping into each of eight large, greased muffin pans. Place slices flat side down in muffin pans. Brush tops with remaining topping mixture.

Bake in 400° oven 15-20 minutes. Sprinkle with sunflower seeds. Makes 8 buns.

Applesauce Puffs

2 cups BISCUIT MIX
¼ cup SUGAR
½ tsp. CINNAMON
¾ cup APPLESAUCE
3 Tbsp. MILK

1 EGG, slightly beaten
2 Tbsp. SALAD OIL
2 Tbsp. melted BUTTER
(or margarine)
¼ cup SUGAR
¼ tsp. CINNAMON

Combine biscuit mix, ¼ cup sugar and ½ teaspoon cinnamon. Add applesauce, milk, egg and oil. Mix until moistened. Fill greased 2″ muffin pans two-thirds full. Bake in 400° oven 12 minutes or until done. Cool slightly; remove. Dip tops in melted butter (or margarine), then in ¼ cup sugar mixed with ¼ teaspoon cinnamon. Makes 12 to 18 puffs.

Apple Cinnamon Waffles

1½ cups FLOUR
½ tsp. SALT
¾ tsp. CINNAMON
1 Tbsp. SUGAR
2 tsp. BAKING POWDER

2 EGGS, separated
1 cup MILK
¾ cup peeled, grated APPLES
¼ cup melted BUTTER
(or margarine)

Sift together flour, salt, cinnamon, sugar and baking powder. Beat egg yolks; add milk. Combine with dry mixture. Add apples and melted butter (or margarine). Beat egg whites until stiff; fold into batter. Bake until golden brown in hot waffle iron. Yields about six waffles.

- **Memo to meal planner:** *If you use a biscuit mix for waffles, simply add cinnamon and grated apple to the package recipe. Pass unsweetened applesauce to dieters who shun syrup.*

Apple Pancakes

1½ cups FLOUR
1½ tsp. BAKING POWDER
¾ tsp. SALT
1 Tbsp. SUGAR

1 EGG, beaten
1¼ cups MILK
2 Tbsp. OIL
¾ cup peeled, grated APPLES

Sift together flour, baking powder, salt and sugar. Combine egg, milk and oil. Add gradually to dry ingredients, stirring only until batter is smooth. Fold in apples.

Drop by spoonfuls onto hot greased griddle. Cook slowly until the surface is covered with bubbles. Turn and cook until the bottom is a delicate brown. Makes about 18 medium-size pancakes.

- **Memo to meal planner:** *You can cut preparation time by using a pancake mix or biscuit mix, following directions on the package for pancakes. Add ¾ to 1 cup of grated apple.*

Apple Muffins

½ cup SUGAR
¼ cup SHORTENING
1 tsp. SALT
1 EGG
1 cup MILK
1½ cups FLOUR
¼ tsp. CINNAMON

3 tsp. BAKING POWDER
1½ cups peeled, chopped
    APPLES
½ cup FLOUR
¼ cup BROWN SUGAR, firmly
    packed (or white sugar)
¼ tsp. CINNAMON

Combine sugar, shortening and salt; add egg and beat well. Stir in milk. Sift together flour, ¼ teaspoon cinnamon and baking powder, then add to other mixture and blend just until flour is moistened. Batter will be lumpy. Add chopped apples which have been coated with ½ cup flour. Blend carefully.

Fill well-greased muffin tins about two-thirds full. Sprinkle with combined brown or white sugar and ¼ teaspoon cinnamon. Bake in 400° oven 20-25 minutes or until golden brown. Makes 12 muffins. Serve warm.

Apple Streusel Muffins

2 cups FLOUR
½ cup SUGAR
3 tsp. BAKING POWDER
1 tsp. SALT
½ cup BUTTER (or margarine)
2 cups peeled, chopped
    APPLES

½ tsp. grated LEMON RIND
1 EGG, beaten
2/3 cup MILK
¼ cup chopped WALNUTS
2 Tbsp. SUGAR
½ tsp. grated LEMON RIND

Sift together flour, ½ cup sugar, baking powder and salt into a large bowl. Cut in butter (or margarine) with a pastry blender until mixture is crumbly. Reserve ½ cup mixture for the streusel topping. Stir apple and ½ teaspoon lemon rind into mixture in bowl. Add milk to egg and add to apple mixture; stir lightly until moist. Spoon into 12 greased muffin cups.

Blend the ½ cup reserved mixture with walnuts, 2 tablespoons sugar and ½ teaspoon lemon rind. Sprinkle over batter in each muffin cup.

Bake in 425° oven 20 minutes or until golden brown. Serve warm. Makes 12 muffins.

Apple Oat Bran Muffins with Raisins

1 cup OAT BRAN
1 cup FLOUR
2 tsp. BAKING POWDER
¼ tsp. CINNAMON
½ tsp. SALT (if desired)
½ tsp. SODA

1 EGG (or 2 whites)
½ cup BROWN SUGAR
1 cup MILK
2 Tbsp. VEGETABLE OIL
1 cup peeled, diced APPLE
½ cup RAISINS

Combine oat bran, flour, baking powder, cinnamon, salt and soda. Beat egg slightly with brown sugar. Add milk and vegetable oil to egg mixture and blend with dry ingredients. Fold in apples and raisins.

Spoon into greased muffin pan for 12 medium muffins. Bake at 400° for about 20 minutes or until tester comes out clean. Leave in muffin pan a few minutes for ease in removing. Serve warm.

Applesauce Honey Rolls

2 loaves (1 lb. each) frozen
 BREAD DOUGH
1 cup BROWN SUGAR,
 firmly packed
½ cup HONEY

3 Tbsp. BUTTER (or margarine)
4 Tbsp. melted BUTTER
 (or margarine)
½ cup APPLESAUCE
2 Tbsp. BROWN SUGAR
¼ cup RAISINS

Allow dough to thaw in plastic bag. Let rise until doubled in bulk.

Mix brown sugar, honey and butter (or margarine). Sprinkle mixture over the bottom of a 13x9″ baking pan.

Place dough on lightly floured pastry board or sheet and roll or pat into a 14x12″ rectangle. Combine 4 tablespoons butter (or margarine), applesauce, 2 tablespoons brown sugar and raisins; spread evenly over dough. Roll and seal. Cut into slices about ½ to 1″ thick. Place slices on honey mixture in pan.

Bake in 350° oven 30 minutes or until golden brown. Cool slighly and turn over onto a plate or tray. Makes 12 rolls.

Apple Doughnuts

1 pkg. active DRY YEAST
½ tsp. SUGAR
¾ cup warm MILK
2 cups FLOUR
2 Tbsp. SUGAR
⅛ tsp. SALT
2 EGGS, beaten
½ cup RAISINS

½ cup peeled, diced APPLES
3 Tbsp. mixed CANDIED FRUIT
1 tsp. grated LEMON PEEL
COOKING OIL
CONFECTIONERS SUGAR

Sprinkle yeast and ½ teaspoon sugar on milk; stir to dissolve. Let stand 10 minutes.

Sift together flour, 2 tablespoons sugar and salt into bowl. Make a well in the center. Add yeast and eggs; mix just until blended. Stir in raisins, apples, candied fruit and lemon peel. Cover and let rise in warm place until doubled, about one hour.

Drop batter by heaping tablespoonfuls into deep hot oil (350°), frying until golden brown, about three minutes. Drain on paper towels. Dust with confectioners sugar. Makes 15.

- *Memo to meal planner: Sugar the doughnuts just before serving by shaking one at a time in a paper bag with granulated or powdered sugar or a mixture of sugar and cinnamon. For a delicious dessert, serve fresh doughnuts with hot applesauce topped with whipped cream or ice cream.*

Apple Doughnut Balls

5 EGGS
2 cups SUGAR
1 cup HEAVY CREAM
1¾ cups BUTTERMILK
1½ cups peeled, grated APPLES
7 cups FLOUR

2 tsp. BAKING SODA
1 tsp. SALT
½ tsp. ground NUTMEG
½ tsp. CINNAMON
1 tsp. VANILLA
COOKING OIL

Beat eggs. Add sugar; beat well. Stir in cream and buttermilk. Add apples. Sift together flour, baking soda, salt, nutmeg and cinnamon. Stir in egg mixture. Add vanilla.

Heat oil to 375°. Drop batter by teaspoonfuls into oil. Fry until brown. Drain on paper towels. Serve plain or sugared. Makes 11 dozen.

Bars and Cookies

Apple Oatmeal Bars

2 cups FLOUR
1 tsp. SALT
1 tsp. BAKING SODA
1 cup BROWN SUGAR,
  firmly packed

1 cup quick-cooking OATMEAL
1 cup SHORTENING
6 Tbsp. BUTTER (or margarine)
4 cups peeled, sliced APPLES
½ cup SUGAR

Sift together flour, salt and baking soda. Add brown sugar and oatmeal; mix well. Cut in shortening until crumbly. Press half of crumbs in greased 13x9x2" baking pan. Dot with 4 tablespoons butter (or margarine). Add apples and sprinkle with ½ cup sugar. Cover with remaining crumb mixture and dot with the remaining 2 tablespoons butter (or margarine).

Bake in 350° oven 40-45 minutes or until done. Makes 2½ dozen.

Applesauce—Orange Bars

½ cup BUTTER (or margarine)
1 cup BROWN SUGAR,
  firmly packed
1 EGG, beaten
¾ cup APPLESAUCE
1 tsp. grated ORANGE PEEL

1 Tbsp. ORANGE JUICE
1½ cups FLOUR
1 tsp. BAKING POWDER
½ tsp. BAKING SODA
½ tsp. SALT
½ cup chopped NUTS

Melt butter (or margarine) in saucepan. Add sugar. Stir in egg, applesauce, orange peel and orange juice. Combine flour, baking powder, salt and soda. Stir in the applesauce mixture and nuts. Spread in a greased 9 x 13" pan. Bake in 350° oven 25 minutes. While warm, spread with glaze. Makes 24-28 servings.

Glaze:

1 cup POWDERED SUGAR

2 Tbsp. ORANGE JUICE

Combine powdered sugar and orange juice and stir until smooth.

Apple Dream Bars

1 cup FLOUR
¼ cup SUGAR
6 Tbsp. BUTTER (or margarine)
2 EGGS
1 cup BROWN SUGAR,
firmly packed
1 tsp. VANILLA

2 cups peeled, diced APPLES
¼ cup chopped ALMONDS
½ cup FLOUR
1 tsp. BAKING POWDER
¼ tsp. SALT
¼ tsp. ground NUTMEG

Combine flour and sugar. Cut in butter until crumbly. Press in 8″ square baking pan.

Bake in 350° oven 20 minutes or until lightly browned.

Beat eggs until thick and lemon-colored. Stir in brown sugar, vanilla, apples and almonds. Sift together flour, baking powder, salt and nutmeg. Stir into egg mixture. Spread over bottom layer.

Bake in 350° oven 30 minutes or until apples are tender and the crust is a golden brown. Makes 16 servings.

- *Memo to meal planner: These bars may also be served as a dessert with whipped cream or ice cream.*

Apple Chip Cookies

1 cup SHORTENING
1½ cups BROWN SUGAR,
firmly packed
¼ cup LIGHT MOLASSES
3 EGGS
3½ cups FLOUR
½ tsp. SALT
1 tsp. BAKING SODA

1 tsp. CINNAMON
¼ tsp. ground CLOVES
¼ tsp. ground NUTMEG
¾ cup chopped WALNUTS
1 cup peeled, finely
chopped APPLES
1 pkg. (6-oz.) semi-sweet
CHOCOLATE CHIPS

Cream together shortening and brown sugar until light and fluffy; add molasses. Add eggs, one at a time, beating well after each addition. Sift together flour, salt, baking soda, cinnamon, cloves and nutmeg. Add to creamed mixture, mixing well. Stir in nuts, apples and chocolate chips. Mix well. Drop by teaspoonfuls on greased baking sheet.

Bake in 350° oven 12-15 minutes, or until done. Makes six dozen.

Oatmeal Apple-Raisin Cookies

1 cup (2 sticks) BUTTER
  (or margarine)
½ cup firmly packed
  BROWN SUGAR
1 cup granulated SUGAR
1 large EGG, beaten
1 tsp. VANILLA

1½ cups FLOUR
1 tsp. SODA
1 tsp. CINNAMON
1½ cups OATMEAL
1 cup peeled, diced APPLES
1 cup RAISINS

Cream butter (or margarine) and the sugars until fluffy. Add the beaten egg, then the vanilla. Sift together the flour, soda and cinnamon and add to creamed mixture. Mix in oatmeal, then the apples and raisins. Refrigerate for an hour.

Drop walnut-size pieces of dough on greased baking sheet, placing far enough apart for cookies to spread. Bake in 350° oven for about 15 minutes or until cookies are set and nicely browned. Makes approximately 60 cookies.

Spicy Apple Squares

1 cup BROWN SUGAR,
  firmly packed
¼ cup BUTTER (or margarine)
1 EGG
½ tsp. VANILLA
¾ cup FLOUR
1 tsp. BAKING POWDER

¼ tsp. SALT
¼ tsp. CINNAMON
½ cup chopped NUTS
1 cup peeled, finely diced
  APPLES
CONFECTIONERS SUGAR

Cream together brown sugar and butter until fluffy. Add egg and vanilla; beat well. Sift together flour, baking powder, salt and cinnamon. Add to creamed mixture; mix well. Add nuts and apples. Spread in well-greased and floured 8″ square baking pan.

Bake in 350° oven 25 minutes or until done. Do not overbake. Cut into squares. Before serving, dust with sifted confectioners sugar. Makes 16 servings.

Apple Chip Oatmeal Cookies

1 cup SHORTENING
1 cup BROWN SUGAR,
  firmly packed
1 cup SUGAR
2 EGGS
1 tsp. VANILLA
1½ cups FLOUR

1 tsp. BAKING SODA
1 tsp. SALT
3 cups quick-cooking OATMEAL
1 cup CHOCOLATE CHIPS
  (or butterscotch)
1 cup peeled, chopped APPLES
½ cup chopped NUTS

Cream together shortening and sugars. Add eggs, one at a time, beating well. Add vanilla. Sift together flour, baking soda and salt. Add to creamed mixture, mixing well. Add oatmeal, chips, apples and nuts. Drop by teaspoonfuls onto greased baking sheet.

Bake in 375° oven 10-12 minutes or until done. Makes about eight dozen.

Apple Cereal Cookies

1 cup BUTTER (or margarine)
1 cup SUGAR
1 cup BROWN SUGAR,
  firmly packed
2 EGGS
1½ cups WHOLE
  WHEAT FLOUR
1½ cups FLOUR
1 tsp. SALT

1 tsp. BAKING SODA
1 tsp. CINNAMON
¼ tsp. ground CLOVES
¼ tsp. ground ALLSPICE
1 cup peeled, grated APPLES
1 cup GRANOLA
1 cup quick-cooking OATMEAL
1 cup RAISINS

Cream together butter (or margarine) and sugars until fluffy. Add eggs, one at a time, beating well. Combine flours, salt, baking soda, cinnamon, cloves and allspice. Add to creamed mixture; mix well. Add grated apple, cereal, oatmeal, and raisins. Drop by teaspoonfuls onto greased baking sheets.

Bake in 350° oven about 15 minutes or until done. Makes about six dozen.

Applesauce Date Nut Cookies

¾ cup BUTTER (or margarine)
½ cup SUGAR
½ cup BROWN SUGAR,
  firmly packed
1 EGG
2 cups FLOUR
1 tsp. BAKING POWDER
½ tsp. BAKING SODA

¼ tsp. SALT
½ tsp. CINNAMON
¼ tsp. ground NUTMEG
1 cup APPLESAUCE
¾ cup cut up DATES
½ cup chopped NUTS
1 tsp. VANILLA

Cream together shortening and sugars until fluffy. Add egg and mix thoroughly. Sift together flour, baking powder, baking soda, salt, cinnamon and nutmeg. Add to creamed mixture alternately with applesauce, blending well. Add dates, nuts and vanilla. Drop by teaspoonfuls on greased baking sheets about 1½ inches apart.

Bake in 400° oven about 10 minutes or until brown. Makes about three dozen cookies.

Apple Nut Bars

3 EGGS
1½ cups SUGAR
1 tsp. VANILLA
1½ cups FLOUR

½ tsp. SALT
3 tsp. BAKING POWDER
3 cups peeled, chopped APPLES
1 cup coarsely chopped NUTS

Beat eggs until foamy, then gradually add sugar, continuing to beat until thick and lemon-colored. Add vanilla. Mix flour, salt and baking powder; blend into egg mixture. Fold in apples and nuts. Spread batter in greased and floured 9x13″ pan. Bake at 350° for 35 minutes or until a pick inserted in the center comes out clean. Makes 24-28 bars.

Apple Walnut Brownies

½ cup BUTTER (or margarine)
2 sq. (1 oz.) UNSWEETENED
  CHOCOLATE
2 EGGS
1 cug SUGAR
1 cup FLOUR

½ tsp. BAKING POWDER
¼ tsp. SALT
1 cup chopped NUTS
1½ cups peeled, finely
  chopped APPLES
1 tsp. VANILLA

Melt butter (or margarine) and chocolate together over hot water. Beat eggs until light and lemon-colored; add sugar gradually while continuing to beat. Stir in the chocolate mixture. Beat for one minute. Sift together flour, baking powder and salt; stir into chocolate mixture. Add nuts, apples and vanilla. Spoon into greased 8" square baking pan.

Bake in 350° oven 35-40 minutes or until done. Makes 16 servings.

Apple Cakes

Baking tips: For best results, always use the pan size given in the recipe. It's always a good idea, too, to test for doneness of the cake, even though baking time is given. Ovens may vary. When the minimum baking time is up, test the cake by inserting a toothpick in the center. If it comes out clean, the cake is done. Also, the cake will shrink slightly from the sides of the pan.

If you use a glass pan, remember to lower the temperature of the oven by 25° from that given in the recipe, but follow the baking time given.

The rack on which the cake is baked should be in the middle of the oven, with the pan centered on that rack. Stagger layer cake pans on the rack so they do not touch each other, and away from the oven walls.

- *Memo to meal planner: Apple cakes freeze very well. Since many of the recipes given here are for large cakes, you may wish to serve half of the freshly baked cake to the family and freeze the other half for later use.*

Autumn Apple Coffee Cake

1 EGG
1/3 cup SUGAR
1 cup FLOUR
1 Tbsp. BAKING POWDER
½ tsp. SALT
½ cup MILK
1 cup quick-cooking OATMEAL

½ cup melted SHORTENING
4 peeled, sliced APPLES
¼ cup SUGAR
½ tsp. CINNAMON
¼ tsp. ground NUTMEG
2 Tbsp. BUTTER (or margarine)

Beat egg and 1/3 cup sugar together until creamy. Sift together flour, baking powder and salt. Add alternately with milk to egg mixture. Stir in oatmeal and melted shortening. Spread half the batter in a greased 9″ round baking pan. Arrange apple slices over batter. Spread remaining batter over apple slices.

Combine ¼ cup sugar, cinnamon and nutmeg. Cut in butter until mixture is crumbly. Sprinkle over batter. Bake in 375° oven 30 minutes or until done. Makes eight servings.

Quick Apple Coffee Cake

2 Tbsp. SUGAR
2 cups BISCUIT MIX
1 EGG
¾ cup MILK
1½ cups peeled, finely
    chopped APPLES
1/3 cup BROWN SUGAR,
    firmly packed

½ tsp. CINNAMON
1/3 cup BISCUIT MIX
¼ cup cold BUTTER
    (or margarine)
½ cup peeled, chopped
    APPLES

Combine sugar, 2 cups biscuit mix, egg, milk and apples; beat vigorously for 30 seconds. Spread batter in greased 9" round baking pan.

Combine brown sugar, cinnamon and 1/3 cup biscuit mix. Cut in butter (or margarine) until crumbly. Add apples. Sprinkle over batter. Bake in 400° oven 25 minutes or until golden brown. Makes 8 to 10 servings.

Spicy Apple Cake

½ cup BUTTER (or margarine)
1 1/3 cups SUGAR
2 EGGS, beaten
1 tsp. SALT
¼ tsp. ground ALLSPICE
¼ tsp. ground NUTMEG
¼ tsp. CINNAMON

2½ cups peeled, chopped
    APPLES
1/3 cup RAISINS
2 cups FLOUR
1 tsp. BAKING POWDER
¼ tsp. BAKING SODA
1/3 cup WATER

Combine ½ cup butter (or margarine), sugar, eggs, salt, allspice, nutmeg and cinnamon. Mix well. Stir in apples and raisins. Sift together flour, baking powder and baking soda. Add to first mixture. Stir in water. Spread in well-greased 9" square baking pan.

Bake in 350° oven 40 minutes or until done.

Topping:

3 Tbsp. BUTTER (or margarine)
¾ cup BROWN SUGAR,
    firmly packed

3 Tbsp. MILK
1¼ tsp. LIGHT CORN SYRUP
1/3 cup chopped NUTS

Combine butter (or margarine), brown sugar, milk and corn syrup in saucepan and bring to a boil. Remove from heat and add nuts. Pour over hot baked cake. Makes 9-12 servings.

Apple Streusel Coffee Cake

Coffee Cake:

2 cups FLOUR
1 cup SUGAR
1 cup SOUR CREAM
½ cup BUTTER (or margarine)
2 EGGS

1 tsp. BAKING POWDER
1 tsp. BAKING SODA
½ tsp. SALT
1 tsp. VANILLA
1 cup peeled, chopped
     APPLES

Streusel:

½ cup BROWN SUGAR
1 tsp. CINNAMON
2 Tbsp. BUTTER (or margarine)
½ cup chopped NUTS

Glaze:

1 cup CONFECTIONERS
     SUGAR
½ tsp. VANILLA
3 to 3½ tsp. MILK

In 3-qt. mixer bowl, combine all coffee cake ingredients *except* apples. Beat at low speed until moistened—about one minute. Continue beating at medium speed, scraping sides of bowl often—about two minutes. Spread half of batter into greased and floured 10-inch bundt pan. Layer with 1/3 cup streusel, chopped apples, 1/3 cup streusel, remaining batter and rest of streusel.

Bake near center of oven at 350° for 40-50 minutes. Cool upright in pan for 15 minutes. Invert on serving plate. Cool completely. Combine glaze ingredients and drizzle glaze over cake. Makes 12 to 16 servings.

Simple Simon Cake

1½ cups FLOUR
¼ cup COCOA
1 cup SUGAR
1 tsp. BAKING SODA
½ tsp. SALT

1 tsp. CIDER VINEGAR
1 tsp. VANILLA
5 Tbsp. OIL
1½ cups APPLESAUCE

Sift together flour, cocoa, sugar, baking soda and salt into greased 8″ square baking pan. Make three depressions in dry ingredients. Pour vinegar into one, vanilla into a second and oil into the third. Spoon applesauce over all. Mix well until smooth.

Bake in 350° oven for 35 minutes. When cool cut into squares. Top with whipped cream or applesauce. Makes eight servings.

Dixie's Fresh Apple Cake

Cake:

2 cups BROWN SUGAR, firmly packed
1 cup BUTTER (or margarine)
2 EGGS
3 cups FLOUR
2 tsp. BAKING SODA
1 tsp. BAKING POWDER
½ tsp. SALT
½ tsp. ground NUTMEG
¼ tsp. ground CLOVES
1 tsp. CINNAMON
1 cup cold COFFEE
2 cups peeled, diced APPLES
1 cup RAISINS
1 cup chopped WALNUTS

Cream together 2 cups brown sugar and butter until fluffy. Add eggs, one at a time, beating after each addition. Sift together flour, baking soda, baking powder, salt, nutmeg, cloves and 1 tsp. cinnamon. Add dry ingredients alternately with the coffee, blending well. Add apples, raisins and walnuts. Spread in greased 13x9x2 baking pan.

Topping:

1/3 cup WHITE SUGAR
3 Tbsp. BROWN SUGAR, firmly packed
½ tsp. CINNAMON
½ cup chopped NUTS

Combine topping ingredients and blend well. Sprinkle topping on batter and gently press into batter. Bake in 350° oven 45 minutes or until done. Makes 20 servings.

Applesauce Chocolate Cup Cakes

½ cup BUTTER (or margarine)
1 cup SUGAR
1 EGG
1¾ cups FLOUR
1 tsp. BAKING SODA
1 tsp. CINNAMON
½ tsp. SALT
½ tsp. BAKING POWDER
¼ tsp. ground ALLSPICE
1½ squares UNSWEETENED CHOCOLATE, grated
1¼ cups APPLESAUCE

Cream together butter (or margarine) and sugar until light. Add egg; beat well. Sift together flour, baking soda, cinnamon, salt, baking powder and allspice. Add chocolate. Add flour mixture alternately with applesauce, beating well each time. Fill paper-lined cupcake pans two-thirds full.

Bake in 375° oven 20 minutes or until done. Makes 18 cupcakes.

Applesauce Date Cake

2 cups FLOUR
2 tsp. BAKING SODA
1 tsp. CINNAMON
½ tsp. ground ALLSPICE
½ tsp. ground NUTMEG
¼ tsp. ground CLOVES
¼ tsp. SALT
2 EGGS

1 cup BROWN SUGAR,
  firmly packed
½ cup BUTTER (or margarine)
2 cups hot APPLESAUCE
1 cup chopped DATES
½ cup chopped WALNUTS

Sift flour with soda, spices and salt. Add eggs, sugar, butter (or margarine) and 1 cup of the hot applesauce. Beat until ingredients are combined. Then beat two minutes longer, occasionally scraping sides of bowl. Add remaining applesauce, the dates and walnuts. Beat one minute. Pour batter into greased and lightly floured 9″ square pan.

Bake in 350° oven 40-50 minutes. Cool in pan 10 minutes. Remove from pan and cool on wire rack. Frost with Cream Cheese Frosting. Makes 9-12 servings.

CREAM CHEESE FROSTING:

1 pkg. (3-oz.) CREAM CHEESE
1 Tbsp. BUTTER (or margarine)

1 tsp. VANILLA
2 cups sifted
  CONFECTIONERS SUGAR

Combine all ingredients and beat until smooth and fluffy. Spread on cake.

• *Memo to meal planner: This is a very rich cake, so make servings small.*

Ginger Apple Upside Down Cake

¼ cup BUTTER (or margarine)
¾ cup BROWN SUGAR,
  firmly packed
3 medium APPLES
1 pkg. (14-oz.) GINGERBREAD
  CAKE MIX

Melt butter (or margarine) in 8″ or 9″ square baking pan. Add brown sugar and stir until dissolved. Peel and core apples. Cut each apple in half to make two thick rings. Arrange rings on butter (or margarine) and sugar mixture.

Prepare cake mix according to package directions. Pour batter over apples.

Bake in 350° oven 40-45 minutes or until done. Cool five minutes; then turn upside down on serving plate. Serve warm with whipped cream. Makes six to eight servings.

Apple Upside Down Cake

3 cups peeled, sliced APPLES
½ cup SUGAR
1 Tbsp. BUTTER (or margarine)
½ tsp. CINNAMON
2 cups FLOUR
2½ tsp. BAKING POWDER
½ tsp. SALT
½ cup SHORTENING
1 cup SUGAR
2 EGGS
1 cup MILK
1 tsp. VANILLA

Grease a 9-inch square pan well. Combine apples, ½ cup sugar, butter and cinnamon in a sauce pan. Cook until tender, stirring frequently. Pour into baking pan.

Combine flour, baking powder and salt. Cream shortening together with sugar. Blend in eggs, one at a time, beating well. Combine milk and vanilla, and add alternately with dry ingredients to creamed mixture, beginning and ending with dry ingredients. Spread over apples in pan.

Bake in 350° oven 35-40 minutes or until done. Remove from oven. Turn cake upside down over serving plate. Let stand a few minutes. Remove pan. Makes 9-12 servings.

- *Memo to meal planner: After turning cake upside down on serving plate, it is VERY IMPORTANT to allow the pan to stand a few minutes before removing it. This cake is especially delicious served warm.*

Sour Cream Apple Cake

3 cups FLOUR
1 cup SUGAR
4 tsp. BAKING POWDER
1 tsp. SALT
1 tsp. CINNAMON
1 cup MILK
½ cup softened BUTTER
   (or margarine)

2 EGGS
2 cups peeled, diced
   APPLES
1 cup dairy SOUR CREAM
2 EGGS, slightly beaten
½ cup SUGAR
1 cup chopped WALNUTS

Sift together flour, sugar, baking powder, salt and cinnamon. Add milk, butter and 2 eggs. Beat until smooth. Stir in apples and pour into greased 13x9x2" baking pan.

Blend together sour cream and 2 eggs. Spread over batter. Sprinkle with combined ½ cup sugar and nuts.

Bake in 375° oven for 30-35 minutes or until done. Makes 16 servings.

Rosy Apple Cake

1 cup SHORTENING
1 cup SUGAR
4 EGGS
1 tsp. VANILLA
2 cups FLOUR
½ tsp. SALT

1 tsp. grated LEMON PEEL
4 cups unpeeled, sliced
   APPLES
½ cup SUGAR
½ tsp. CINNAMON
4 Tbsp. BUTTER (or margarine)

Cream together shortening and 1 cup of sugar until light and fluffy. Beat in eggs, one at a time, beating well after each addition. Add vanilla. Sift together flour and salt; add grated lemon peel. Beat well. Spread into greased 13x9x2" baking pan.

Place apples in rows on batter. Combine ½ cup sugar and cinnamon; sprinkle over apples. Dot with butter (or margarine).

Bake in 350° oven for 40-45 minutes or until done. Makes 16 servings.

- **Memo to meal planner:** *Don't be confused by the ingredients. The batter does not contain baking powder or liquids. With its rows of red apple slices, this is an attractive cake.*

Applesauce Cake with Apple Juice Frosting

1 pkg. (18½-oz.) YELLOW
  CAKE MIX
½ tsp. ground NUTMEG
½ tsp. ground ALLSPICE

1 tsp. CINNAMON
1½ cups APPLESAUCE
2 EGGS
¾ cup chopped WALNUTS

Combine cake mix, nutmeg, allspice and cinnamon. Add applesauce and eggs. Beat three minutes, until smooth and creamy. Stir in chopped walnuts. Pour into two greased and floured 8″ layer cake pans.

Bake in 350° oven 25-30 minutes or until cake tests done. Cool and frost with Fluffy Apple Juice Frosting. Makes 16 servings.

FLUFFY APPLE JUICE FROSTING

1½ cups SUGAR
¾ cup APPLE JUICE

⅛ tsp. SALT
3 EGG WHITES

Mix sugar, apple juice and salt in two-quart saucepan. Cook until the syrup forms a soft ball (234° to 240°) when a little of the mixture is dropped into a cup of cold water. Pour very slowly over stiffly beaten egg whites, beating constantly. Continue beating until mixture stands in soft peaks. Spread between layers and over the top and sides of cake.

Finnish Apple Sugar Cake

¼ cup BUTTER (or margarine)
1 cup SUGAR
2 EGGS
2 cups FLOUR
1½ tsp. BAKING POWDER

¼ tsp. SALT
¾ cup LIGHT CREAM
2 cups peeled, sliced
  APPLES
3 Tbsp. SUGAR
1 tsp. CINNAMON

Cream together butter and 1 cup sugar thoroughly. Add eggs, beat until light and fluffy. Sift flour with baking powder and salt; add alternately with cream. Mix until batter is smooth. Spread in well-greased 9″ square baking pan. Place apple slices in rows over cake with outer edges up. Combine 3 tablespoons sugar and cinnamon; sprinkle evenly over the cake.

Bake in 350° oven 40-45 minutes or until done. Makes nine servings.

Em's Eggless Applesauce Fruit Cake

3 cups strained APPLESAUCE
   (sweetened or unsweetened)
1 cup SHORTENING
2 cups SUGAR
4½ cups FLOUR
4 tsp. BAKING SODA
1 tsp. ground NUTMEG
2½ tsp. CINNAMON
½ tsp. ground CLOVES
1 tsp. SALT
1 lb. pitted & chopped DATES
1 lb. chopped RAISINS
¼ lb. each of chopped NUTS,
   CANDIED CHERRIES,
   PINEAPPLE and CITRON

Boil together for five minutes the applesauce, shortening and sugar. Let stand overnight or at least eight hours.

Sift together flour, soda, spices and salt. Dredge the chopped fruits and nuts with sifted flour mixture. Mix all ingredients together thoroughly.

Bake in two pans lined with waxed paper or foil in a very slow oven (250°) until cake tests done. A bread tin, 8″ by 4″ takes about two hours, depending on the amount of fruit added. Fill pans about two-thirds full. Makes two cakes.

- *Memo to meal planner: The large amount of baking soda— 4 teaspoons—is correct for this recipe.*

Cocoa Apple Cake

1 cup BUTTER (or margarine)
2 cups SUGAR
3 EGGS
½ cup cold WATER
2½ cups FLOUR
2 Tbsp. COCOA
1 tsp. CINNAMON
½ tsp. ALLSPICE
1 tsp. BAKING SODA
½ cup CHOCOLATE CHIPS
1 cup chopped NUTS
2 cups peeled, chopped or
   grated APPLES
½ tsp. VANILLA

Preheat oven to 325°. Grease and flour a 10″ tube pan.

Cream butter (or margarine) and sugar. Add eggs one at a time, beating well after each addition. Add water. Mix. Sift together flour and remaining dry ingredients. Add and mix. (Do NOT over-mix.) Add remaining ingredients. Pour into tube pan. Bake at 325° for 60-70 minutes. Cool upright on a rack 10-15 minutes. Invert and remove from pan and finish cooling on a rack. Makes 12 to 16 servings.

Apple Lemon Sauce Cake

½ cup BUTTER (or margarine)
2 cups SUGAR
2 EGGS
2½ cups FLOUR
2 tsp. BAKING SODA
1 tsp. CINNAMON
½ tsp. ground NUTMEG

½ tsp. SALT
⅛ tsp. ground CLOVES
4 cups peeled, grated
   APPLES
1 cup chopped NUTS
1 cup RAISINS

Cream together butter (or margarine) and sugar until light. Add eggs; beat well. Sift together flour, baking soda, cinnamon, nutmeg, salt and cloves. Add alternately with grated apple, mixing well after each addition. Blend in nuts and raisins. Spread in greased 13x9x2″ baking pan.

Bake in 350° oven 45 minutes or until done. Serve warm with Lemon Sauce over cake. Makes 16 servings.

LEMON SAUCE:

4 tsp. CORNSTARCH
½ cup SUGAR
⅛ tsp. SALT
¼ tsp. NUTMEG

1 cup WATER
1 tsp. grated LEMON PEEL
2 Tbsp. LEMON JUICE
2 Tbsp. BUTTER (or margarine)

Mix cornstarch, sugar, salt and nutmeg in a small saucepan. Gradually stir in water. Cook, stirring constantly, until mixture thickens and boils. Boil and stir one minute. Remove from heat. Stir in lemon peel, lemon juice and butter (or margarine).

Apple Whole Wheat Cake

1 cup SHORTENING
1 cup BROWN SUGAR,
  firmly packed
1 cup SUGAR
3 EGGS
1 cup WHOLE WHEAT FLOUR
1 cup FLOUR
3 tsp. BAKING POWDER
½ tsp. SALT
¾ cup MILK
¼ cup cold COFFEE
3 cups peeled, sliced
  APPLES
1/3 cup SUGAR
½ tsp. CINNAMON

Cream together shortening, brown sugar and 1 cup sugar until light. Add eggs, one at a time, beating well after each addition. Sift together flours, baking powder and salt. Add flour mixture alternately with the milk and coffee. (Do NOT overbeat!) Place half of mixture in greased and lightly floured 13x9x2" baking pan. Place half the apple slices in about three rows on top. Add the remaining batter and then the rest of the apple slices. Sprinkle with combined 1/3 cup sugar and ½ teaspoon cinnamon.

Bake in 350° oven 40-45 minutes or until done. Makes 16 servings.

Apple Blueberry Cake

½ cup BUTTER (or margarine)
1½ cups SUGAR
3 EGGS
2½ cups FLOUR
1½ tsp. BAKING POWDER
1 tsp. BAKING SODA
½ tsp. SALT
1 cup dairy SOUR CREAM
1 tsp. VANILLA
1 tsp. ground CARDAMOM
1 cup APPLESAUCE
1 cup BLUEBERRIES
1/3 cup BROWN SUGAR,
  loosely packed
1 Tbsp. FLOUR

Cream together butter (or margarine) and sugar until fluffy. Add eggs one at a time, beating well after each addition. Sift together flour, baking powder, baking soda and salt. Add to creamed mixture, alternating with the sour cream. Gently stir in vanilla, cardamom and applesauce. Combine blueberries, brown sugar and 1 tablespoon flour. Pour half the batter into a well-greased and lightly floured 13x9x2" baking pan. Cover with blueberry mixture. Top with remaining batter. Bake in 350° oven 35-40 minutes or until done. Makes 16-20 servings.

Easy Apple Spice Cake

1 pkg. (18½-oz.) SPICE
   CAKE MIX
2/3 cup WATER
1 EGG
¼ tsp. CINNAMON

¼ cup BUTTER (or margarine),
   melted
1 tsp. VANILLA
2 cups peeled, sliced APPLES
2 Tbsp. BUTTER (or margarine)

Blend half a package (approximately 2¼ cups) cake mix, water and egg in mixing bowl. Beat at medium speed until batter is smooth. Pour half the batter into a greased 9" square pan. Combine remaining cake mix with cinnamon; add melted butter (or margarine) and vanilla. Toss with a fork to form large crumbs.

Sprinkle half of crumb mixture over batter in pan. Arrange 1 cup of apple slices over crumb mixture. Carefully spoon on remaining batter. Arrange rest of apple slices over batter. Dot with the butter and sprinkle with remaining crumb mixture.

Bake in 350° oven 40-45 minutes or until done. Serve warm. Makes nine servings.

Fresh Fruit Cake

2 cups APPLES (peeled, cored
   and cubed)
2 cups PEARS (peeled, cored
   and cubed)
1½ cups whole CRANBERRIES
   (drained and patted dry)
½ cup (1 stick) softened
   BUTTER (or margarine)

1¼ cups SUGAR
4 EGGS
2½ cups FLOUR
½ tsp. BAKING SODA
1 Tbsp. BAKING POWDER
1/3 cup BUTTERMILK
1 tsp. VANILLA
¼ cup FLOUR

Preheat oven to 350°. Butter and flour a 10" tube pan. Cream butter and sugar. Add eggs one at a time and beat until light. Sift flour, soda and baking powder together. Mix half the flour mixture into the batter. Add buttermilk. Blend. Add the remaining flour and mix until blended. Add vanilla.

Combine apples, pears, cranberries and one-fourth cup flour. Stir gently into the batter. Pour into prepared pan. Bake about 60-65 minutes. Cool 10-15 minutes in the pan on a rack. Do not invert. Remove from pan and cool completely on a wire rack. Serves 12-16

- **Memo to meal planner:** *As this is a very moist cake, refrigerate or freeze. Wrap carefully.*

Apple Pies

Pastry for 1-Crust (8" or 9" pie)

1 cup FLOUR
½ tsp. SALT

1/3 cup plus 2 to 3 Tbsp.
  SHORTENING
2 to 3 Tbsp. WATER

Combine flour and salt in bowl. Cut in shortening until particles are size of peas. Sprinkle mixture with water, a tablespoon at a time, tossing together with flour until flour is moistened. Form into a ball. Roll out on floured surface to fit either 8" or 9" pie pan.

Pastry for a 2-Crust 9" Pie

2 cups FLOUR
  (spooned into cup)
1 tsp. SALT

¾ cup SHORTENING
  (hydrogenated vegetable)
4 to 6 Tbsp. WATER

Combine flour and salt, and cut in the shortening. When the particles are the size of peas, sprinkle with water, a tablespoon at a time, tossing together with a fork until all the flour is moistened. Gather the dough together and form into two balls. Roll out to fit 9" pie pan. Make several slits near center of top crust to allow steam to escape.

- ***Memo to meal planner:*** *If you wish a truly rich pie crust which melts in your mouth, use 1 cup hydrogenated vegetable shortening instead of ¾ cup. The recipe given makes two crusts.*

Old Fashioned Apple Pie

6 to 8 medium tart pie APPLES (6 to 7 cups apples, peeled and sliced)
¾ to 1 cup SUGAR

¼ tsp. CINNAMON (optional)
2 Tbsp. BUTTER (or margarine)

Peel, core and slice apples into mixing bowl. Combine sugar and cinnamon, and add to apples. Stir gently with a rubber spatula until all apples are coated with sugar. Fill a 9" pastry-lined pan. Dot with butter (or margarine). Cover with top crust. Cut vents. Flute the edges.

Bake in a hot oven (400°) for 45-50 minutes until top crust is golden brown and apples are tender. Makes six to eight servings.

• *Memo to meal planner: Serve warm or cold. Follow the practice of Colonial days and serve with a slice of cheese. Or for a special dessert, top with cinnamon ice cream.*

If you use apples right from the tree, they are very juicy, so you may have to use a tablespoon of flour. Add it to the sugar and combine with the apples.

Apple Blueberry Pie

Unbaked 8" PIE SHELL
3 cups peeled, sliced APPLES
1 cup BLUEBERRIES, fresh or frozen and thawed

1 cup SUGAR
1½ Tbsp. CORNSTARCH
½ tsp. CINNAMON

Combine apples, blueberries, sugar, cornstarch and cinnamon; mix well. Turn into pie shell and sprinkle on cheese crumb topping.

Bake in 425° oven 40-50 minutes or until apples are tender. Makes six servings.

CHEESE CRUMB TOPPING:

1 cup FLOUR
2 Tbsp. SUGAR

3 Tbsp. BUTTER (or margarine)
½ cup shredded CHEDDAR CHEESE

Combine all ingredients; mix until crumbly.

Danish Pastry Apple Squares

3 cups FLOUR
1 tsp. SALT
1¼ cups SHORTENING
1 EGG YOLK
Enough MILK to make ¾ cup
  with the egg yolk

1 cup crushed CORN FLAKES
8 cups peeled, sliced APPLES
2/3 cup SUGAR
½ tsp. CINNAMON
1 EGG WHITE

Mix flour and salt, and blend in shortening until crumbly. Add the egg yolk and milk for the pie crust.

Divide dough into two parts. Roll half of dough to fit a 10½x15½x1" jelly roll pan or cookie sheet. Sprinkle bottom crust with crushed corn flakes. Combine sugar and cinnamon and add to apples, stirring gently. Spread apple mixture over bottom crust on top of corn flakes. Roll out other half of dough and place on top. Pinch edges together to seal. Beat egg white stiff and brush over top crust. Bake at 400° for 50-60 minutes or until golden.

FROSTING:

1 cup CONFECTIONERS
  SUGAR

½ tsp. VANILLA
1 to 2 Tbsp. WATER

While pie squares are baking, mix together the ingredients for the frosting. Remove pie squares from oven at end of baking period and cool slightly. Frost when crust is still warm.

- *Memo to meal planner: For a dessert, cut into 16 pieces and serve with a fork. For finger food, cut into 36 bars. Oatmeal may be substituted for the corn flakes.*

Apple Ice Cream Pie

Baked 9" PIE SHELL
¾ cup APPLE JUICE
1 pkg. (3-oz.) LEMON GELATIN

1 pt. Vanilla ICE CREAM
1½ cups APPLESAUCE

Bring apple juice to a boil. Remove from heat and stir in gelatin. Stir until dissolved. Add ice cream and stir until melted. Blend in applesauce. Chill until mixture begins to thicken. Turn into pie shell. Chill until set. Makes six to eight servings.

Apple Cream Pie

QUICK PASTRY
2½ cups peeled, sliced APPLES
½ cup SUGAR
¼ cup FLOUR
⅛ tsp. ground NUTMEG
1 cup HEAVY CREAM

Prepare Quick Pastry.

Combine apples, sugar, flour and nutmeg. Turn into pastry-lined pie pan.

Bake in 375° oven 10 minutes. Pour cream over all. Bake 30-35 minutes or until apples are tender. Makes six to eight servings.

QUICK PASTRY:

1½ cups FLOUR
2 Tbsp. SUGAR
⅛ tsp. SALT
½ cup BUTTER (or margarine)
3 EGG YOLKS
1 Tbsp. WATER

Sift together flour, sugar and salt. Cut in butter (or margarine) until crumbly. Combine egg yolks and water. Add to crumb mixture and mix well. Knead until smooth. Pat into 9″ pie pan with fingers. Flute edges.

- *Memo to meal planner: This pie is for you if you dislike rolling pastry. Just pat it in the pan. Do not freeze this pie.*

French Apple Pie

Unbaked 9″ PIE SHELL
7 cups peeled, sliced APPLES
2/3 cup SUGAR
½ tsp. CINNAMON
1½ Tbsp. BUTTER
(or margarine)

Combine apples, sugar and cinnamon; mix well. Turn into pie shell. Dot with butter (or margarine). Sprinkle with Topping.

Bake in 400° oven 50 minutes or until apples are tender. Serve warm. Makes six to eight servings.

TOPPING:

1 cup FLOUR
½ cup BROWN SUGAR,
  firmly packed
¼ tsp. CINNAMON
½ cup BUTTER (or margarine)

Combine flour, sugar and cinnamon. Cut in butter until crumbly.

Apple Pear Crumb Pie

Unbaked 9" PIE SHELL
2 cups peeled, diced APPLES
3½ cups canned PEARS,
  drained and sliced
1/3 cup SUGAR
2 Tbsp. FLOUR

¼ tsp. SALT
¼ tsp. CINNAMON
½ cup RAISINS
1 Tbsp. LEMON JUICE
2 Tbsp. BUTTER (or margarine)

Combine apples, pears, sugar, flour, salt, cinnamon, raisins and lemon juice; mix well. Turn into pie shell. Dot with butter (or margarine). Sprinkle with Crumb Topping.

Bake in 450° oven 10 minutes. Cover with aluminum foil and continue baking at 350° 40 minutes or until apples are tender. Serve warm. Makes six to eight servings.

CRUMB TOPPING:

¼ cup FLOUR
½ cup BROWN SUGAR
¼ tsp. SALT

1 pkg. (3-oz.) CREAM CHEESE
½ cup chopped WALNUTS

Combine flour, sugar and salt. Cut in cheese until crumbly. Stir in walnuts.

Apple Crumb Pie with Yogurt

Unbaked 9" PIE SHELL
¾ cup SUGAR
¼ cup BROWN SUGAR,
  firmly packed
2 Tbsp. FLOUR
½ tsp. CINNAMON
¼ tsp. ground NUTMEG
1 tsp. LEMON JUICE

¾ cup plain or vanilla
  YOGURT
6 cups peeled, sliced
  APPLES
½ cup FLOUR
½ cup BROWN SUGAR,
  firmly packed
¼ cup BUTTER (or margarine)

Combine sugar, ¼ cup brown sugar, 2 tablespoons flour, cinnamon, nutmeg, lemon juice and yogurt; blend well. Stir in apples. Turn into pie shell.

Combine ½ cup flour and ½ cup brown sugar. Cut in butter (or margarine) until crumbly. Sprinkle over apple mixture.

Bake in 350° oven 50 minutes or until apples are tender. Makes six to eight servings.

Gourmet Apple Pie

Unbaked 9" PIE SHELL
1 Tbsp. DRY BREAD CRUMBS
1 Tbsp. chopped, toasted
  ALMONDS
5 cups peeled, sliced APPLES
1 EGG
1 EGG YOLK

1 cup HEAVY CREAM
½ cup SUGAR
¼ tsp. CINNAMON
⅛ tsp. ground NUTMEG
1½ Tbsp. melted BUTTER
  (or margarine)
3 Tbsp. SUGAR

Sprinkle bread crumbs and almonds in pie shell. Arrange apples in pie shell but don't heap apples. Bake in 350° oven five minutes.

Combine egg and extra yolk. Beat slightly. Blend in cream, sugar, cinnamon and nutmeg. Pour half of this cream mixture over the apples. Continue baking for 30 minutes or until custard is firm. Pour remaining cream mixture over all. Bake 30 or more minutes or until knife inserted near the edge comes out clean. Remove from oven.

Pour melted butter (or margarine) over the top and sprinkle with 3 tablespoons sugar. Return to oven long enough to glaze topping, about eight minutes. Cool before cutting. Makes six to eight servings.

Sour Cream Apple Pie

Unbaked 9" PIE SHELL
2 Tbsp. FLOUR
⅛ tsp. SALT
¾ cup SUGAR
1 EGG
1 cup dairy SOUR CREAM

1 tsp. VANILLA
¼ tsp. ground NUTMEG
2 cups peeled, sliced
  APPLES

Combine flour, salt, sugar, egg, sour cream, vanilla and nutmeg; beat well. Stir in apples. Pour into pie shell.

Bake in 400° oven 15 minutes. Reduce oven to 350° and bake 30 minutes longer. Remove from oven; sprinkle with Nut Topping. Return to oven 10 minutes or until lightly browned. Makes six to eight servings.

NUT TOPPING:

¼ cup SUGAR
¼ cup FLOUR
¾ tsp. CINNAMON

¼ cup chopped NUTS
¼ cup BUTTER (or margarine)

Combine all ingredients and mix until crumbly.

Apple Pizza Pie

1¼ cups FLOUR
1 tsp. SALT
½ cup SHORTENING
1 cup shredded CHEDDAR
   CHEESE
¼ cup iced WATER
½ cup POWDERED NON-
   DAIRY CREAMER
½ cup BROWN SUGAR,
   firmly packed

½ cup SUGAR
1/3 cup FLOUR
¼ tsp. SALT
1 tsp. CINNAMON
½ tsp. ground NUTMEG
¼ cup BUTTER (or margarine)
6 cups peeled, sliced
   APPLES (½" thick)
2 Tbsp. LEMON JUICE

Combine 1¼ cups flour and 1 teaspoon salt. Cut in shortening until crumbly. Add cheese. Sprinkle water over mixture gradually; shape into a ball. Roll pastry into 15" circle on floured surface. Place on baking sheet; turn up ¼" rim.

Combine creamer, brown sugar, sugar, 1/3 cup flour, ¼ teaspoon salt, cinnamon and nutmeg. Sprinkle half of this mixture over pastry. Cut batter into remaining mixture until crumbly; set aside.

Arrange apple slices in circles on crust, overlapping the slices. Sprinkle with lemon juice and crumb mixture.

Bake in 450° oven 30 minutes or until apples are tender. Serve warm. Makes 12 servings.

Apple Cranberry Relish Pie

Unbaked 9" PIE SHELL
6 cups peeled, sliced
   APPLES
1/3 cup CRANBERRY RELISH,
   canned or frozen (thawed)

¾ cup SUGAR
1½ Tbsp. CORNSTARCH
⅛ tsp. CINNAMON

Combine apples, cranberry relish, sugar, cornstarch and cinnamon. Turn into pie shell.

Bake in 400° oven 45 minutes or until apples are tender. Makes six to eight servings.

Cranberry Apple Pie

ORANGE PASTRY
1 cup CRANBERRIES
3 cups peeled, sliced
APPLES

1 cup SUGAR
2 Tbsp. FLOUR
⅛ tsp. SALT
2 Tbsp. BUTTER (or margarine)

Prepare Orange Pastry.

Combine cranberries, apples, sugar, flour and salt; mix well. Turn into pastry-lined pie pan. Cover with top crust. Cut vents in top. Flute edges.

Bake in 400° oven 50 minutes or until apples are tender. Makes six to eight servings.

ORANGE PASTRY:

2 cups FLOUR
1 tsp. SALT
2/3 cup SHORTENING

1 tsp. grated ORANGE PEEL
1/3 cup ORANGE JUICE

Sift flour and salt. Cut in shortening until crumbly. Add orange peel and orange juice. Toss together with fork until flour is moistened. Form into a ball. Divide in half. Roll out one half on floured surface to fit 9" pie pan.

Glossy Apple Raisin Pie

PASTRY for 2-CRUST 9" PIE
6 cups peeled, sliced APPLES
¾ cup SUGAR
2 Tbsp. FLOUR
½ tsp. CINNAMON

¼ tsp. SALT
½ cup RAISINS
2 Tbsp. ORANGE JUICE
¼ cup BUTTER (or margarine

Combine apples, sugar, flour, cinnamon, salt and raisins; mix well. Turn into pastry-lined pie pan. Sprinkle with orange juice; dot with butter. Place top crust over filling. Cut vents; flute edges.

Bake in 400° oven 40 minutes or until apples are tender. Spread Orange Glaze over hot pie. Makes six to eight servings.

ORANGE GLAZE:

1 cup sifted CONFECTIONERS
SUGAR

3 Tbsp. ORANGE JUICE
1 tsp. grated ORANGE PEEL

Combine all ingredients and mix until smooth.

Apple Pumpkin Pie

PASTRY for TWO
  8" PIE SHELLS
4 cups peeled, sliced APPLES
2/3 cup SUGAR
3 Tbsp. FLOUR
2 cups canned PUMPKIN
½ cup SUGAR
½ cup BROWN SUGAR,
  firmly packed
¼ tsp. ground CLOVES
1 tsp. CINNAMON
½ tsp. ground NUTMEG
¼ tsp. ground GINGER
2 EGGS, beaten
1½ cups EVAPORATED MILK
1 Tbsp. BUTTER (or margarine)

Combine apples, sugar and flour; mix well. Combine pumpkin, ½ cup sugar, brown sugar, cloves, cinnamon, nutmeg, ginger and eggs; blend well. Heat evaporated milk and butter (or margarine) until butter (or margarine) is melted. Add to pumpkin mixture; blend well. Stir in apple mixture. Pour mixture into pie shells.

Bake in 425° oven 10 minutes. Reduce temperature to 350° and continue baking 40 minutes or until knife inserted at edge of filling comes out clean. Makes 12 servings.

Upside Down Apple Pecan Pie

PASTRY for 2-CRUST 9" PIE
¼ cup soft BUTTER
  (or margarine)
1/3 cup PECAN HALVES
2/3 cup BROWN SUGAR,
  firmly packed
6 cups peeled, sliced APPLES
1 Tbsp. LEMON JUICE
1 Tbsp. FLOUR
½ cup SUGAR
½ tsp. CINNAMON
¼ tsp. SALT

Spread butter evenly on bottom and sides of 9" pie pan. Press pecan halves, rounded side down, into butter (or margarine). Sprinkle brown sugar evenly over pecans.

Roll out ½ of pastry. Place over mixture in pan, trimming edges evenly.

Combine apples, lemon juice, flour, sugar, cinnamon and salt. Arrange in crust. Top with remaining pastry. Flute edges and cut vents in top.

Bake in 350° oven one hour or until apples are tender. Remove from oven when syrup stops bubbling. Place serving plate over pie and invert. Remove pie pan. Makes six to eight servings.

Recipe Notes

Apple Desserts

Baked Apples

Select good quality baking apples of uniform size. Wash apples and remove core, but do not cut through to the blossom end. Peel the upper third or fourth of the stem end. Place in DEEP BAKING DISH.

In center of EACH apple put 1 to 2 tablespoons of granulated sugar, brown sugar, maple syrup OR honey AND ½ teaspoon butter or margarine. Sprinkle apples with cinnamon or nutmeg.

Pour 1 cup of water around the apples (or to the depth of ½"). Cover with aluminum foil and bake at 350° for 45-60 minutes. Serve warm or cold. (Also see Microwave recipe.)

- *Memo to meal planner: Vary baked apples with one of these fillings:*

  - *Chopped dates with chopped walnuts, almonds or pecans*
  - *Raisins*
  - *Cranberry sauce or cranberry relish*
  - *Mincemeat*
  - *Chopped figs and nuts*
  - *Orange marmalade*

Amber Apples

2 lbs. firm APPLES
(About 6 medium)

1 can (46-oz.) APPLE JUICE
Vanilla ICE CREAM

Peel and core apples. Cut into eighths.

Pour apple juice in a large skillet. Add apples in a single layer. Cook very slowly, basting occasionally, until apples are translucent and a deep amber color. Add a little water or more juice if syrup becomes too thick.

Lift slices carefully from juice and arrange in a glass serving dish. Chill and serve with vanilla ice cream. Makes six servings.

Apple Coconut Dessert

7½ cups peeled, sliced
  APPLES
½ cup BROWN SUGAR
  firmly packed
1½ tsp. CINNAMON
¼ tsp. ground MACE
3 Tbsp. FLOUR

¼ cup ORANGE JUICE
½ cup BROWN SUGAR,
  firmly packed
1/3 cup FLOUR
6 Tbsp. BUTTER (or margarine)
½ cup COCONUT

Arrange apples in greased 8" square baking pan. Combine ½ cup brown sugar, cinnamon, mace and 3 tablespoons flour; mix well. Sprinkle over apples. Pour orange juice evenly over all.

Combine ½ cup brown sugar and 1/3 cup flour. Cut in butter (or margarine) until crumbly. Stir in coconut. Sprinkle over apples. Cover with aluminum foil.

Bake in 425° oven 20 minutes. Remove foil; bake 15 more minutes. Makes six to eight servings.

Creamy Apple Cheese Dessert

1 cup FLOUR
1 Tbsp. SUGAR
⅛ tsp. SALT
¼ cup BUTTER (or margarine)
1 EGG YOLK, beaten
1 tsp. WATER
2½ cups canned APPLE
  SLICES, drained
1/3 cup SUGAR

¼ tsp. CINNAMON
¼ tsp. ground NUTMEG
1 pkg (3-oz.) CREAM CHEESE,
  softened
½ cup SUGAR
2 EGGS, beaten
⅛ tsp. SALT
½ cup HEAVY CREAM
1 tsp. VANILLA

Combine flour, 1 tablespoon sugar and ⅛ teaspoon salt. Cut in butter (or margarine) until crumbly. Combine 1 egg yolk and water; stir into crumb mixture. Press in bottom and sides of 8" square baking pan.

Combine apples, 1/3 cup sugar, cinnamon and nutmeg; mix well. Arrange apples in crust. Bake in 425° oven 10 minutes.

Whip cream cheese until smooth. Beat in ½ cup sugar, 2 eggs and ⅛ teaspoon salt. Blend in cream and vanilla; mix well. Pour evenly over apples.

Reduce oven to 350°. Bake 30-35 minutes more or until set. Cool and then chill. Serve with whipped cream. Makes eight servings.

Apple Crisp

6 to 8 peeled APPLES,
  sliced thickly
1 cup SUGAR
  (brown or half white)

¾ cup FLOUR
1 tsp. CINNAMON
½ cup BUTTER (or margarine)

Place sliced apples in 8x8″ greased pan. Blend sugar, flour and cinnamon. Work in the butter (or margarine) until the mixture is crumbly. Pack mixture closely over the apples. If apples seem very dry, add a little water. Bake 45 minutes to an hour at 375°. Serves six. (Also see Microwave recipe.)

Apple Cheese Crisp

6½ cups peeled, sliced
  APPLES
1 cup SUGAR
½ cup FLOUR
¼ tsp. SALT

⅛ tsp. CINNAMON
¼ cup BUTTER (or margarine)
2/3 cup shredded CHEDDAR
  CHEESE

Arrange apples in 9″ pie plate. Sprinkle with ½ cup sugar. Combine remaining ½ cup sugar, flour, salt and cinnamon. Cut in butter until crumbly. Add cheese; mix well. Sprinkle over apples.

Bake in 350° oven 40-45 minutes or until apples are tender. Serve warm or cold. Makes six to eight servings.

Apple Cranberry Crisp

4½ cups peeled, sliced
  APPLES
¾ cup whole CRANBERRY
  SAUCE
¾ cup FLOUR

1 cup BROWN SUGAR,
  firmly packed
1 tsp. CINNAMON
6 Tbsp. BUTTER (or margarine)

Arrange apples in greased 8″ baking dish. Spread cranberry sauce on top. Combine flour, brown sugar and cinnamon. Cut in butter (or margarine) until crumbly. Sprinkle over apple mixture.

Bake in 350° oven 35-40 minutes or until apples are tender. Serve warm or cold. Makes six to eight servings.

Oatmeal Apple Crunch

6 cups peeled, sliced
   APPLES
1 cup FLOUR
1 cup BROWN SUGAR,
   firmly packed

¼ tsp. CINNAMON
1 cup BUTTER (or margarine)
1 cup quick-cooking OATMEAL
¼ cup chopped WALNUTS

Arrange apples in greased 8" square baking dish. Combine flour, brown sugar and cinnamon. Cut in butter until crumbly. Add oatmeal and walnuts; mix well. Sprinkle over apples.

Bake in 350° oven 50-60 minutes or until apples are tender. Serve warm. Makes nine servings.

Apple Graham Cracker Delight

16 GRAHAM CRACKERS
APPLESAUCE

WHIPPED CREAM

Use 4 graham crackers for each serving. Spread a generous amount of applesauce on 3 of the crackers. Stack them like a layer cake. Frost outside of stack with whipped cream. Chill at least 20 minutes. Makes four servings.

Apple Macaroon Dessert

4 cups peeled, sliced
   APPLES
½ cup SUGAR
½ tsp. CINNAMON
½ cup chopped PECANS
½ cup COCONUT
½ cut BUTTER (or margarine)

½ cup SUGAR
1 EGG, beaten
¾ cup FLOUR
½ tsp. VANILLA
Sweetened WHIPPED CREAM

Arrange apples in 9" pie plate. Combine ½ cup sugar and cinnamon; sprinkle over apples. Top with pecans and coconut.

Cream butter (or margarine) until fluffy. Gradually beat in ½ cup sugar. Add egg, flour and vanilla; mix well. Spread over apple mixture.

Bake in 350° oven 30-35 minutes or until top is golden brown. Serve warm or cold with whipped cream. Makes eight servings.

Apple Batter Pudding

PUDDING:

3 cups APPLES, peeled and
   cut in small pieces
½ cup SUGAR

1 Tbsp. BUTTER (or margarine)
¼ cup hot WATER

Place the apples in a 1½-quart casserole or 8x8″ pan. Sprinkle sugar over apples, dot with the butter (or margarine) and pour hot water over apples. Add the batter.

BATTER:

2 EGGS
½ cup SUGAR
2 Tbsp. melted BUTTER
   (or margarine)

½ cup FLOUR
2 tsp. BAKING POWDER
½ tsp. SALT

Beat eggs and sugar together, add the melted butter (or margarine). Sift together flour, baking powder and salt and add to egg mixture. Pour batter over the apples. Bake 40 minutes in 350° oven. To serve, spoon out of casserole or cut into squares. Makes about six to eight servings.

Apple Pudding Dessert

LOWER CRUST:

1 cup BUTTER (or margarine)
2 cups FLOUR

2 Tbsp. SUGAR

Blend butter (or margarine), flour and sugar. Pat into a 9x13″ pan.

FILLING:

12 to 14 medium-size
   tart APPLES
1 cup SUGAR

1 tsp. CINNAMON
1 pkg. (3-oz.) INSTANT
   VANILLA PUDDING

Peel, core and slice apples into crust. Combine sugar and cinnamon and sprinkle over apples. Bake at 400° for 30 minutes. Prepare instant pudding. Pour prepared instant pudding over apples while they are still hot. Refrigerate. Serve with whipped cream. Makes 16 servings.

Apple Pudding Pie

1 cup SUGAR
¼ cup BUTTER (or margarine)
1 EGG
1 cup FLOUR
¼ tsp. SALT
1 tsp. BAKING SODA
1 tsp. CINNAMON

1 tsp. ground NUTMEG
2 Tbsp. hot WATER
1 tsp. VANILLA
2½ cups APPLES,
  peeled and diced
½ cup chopped NUTS

Cream together the butter (or margarine) and sugar; add the egg and beat well. Sift together the flour, salt, soda and spices. Add to the creamed mixture alternately with the hot water. Stir in the vanilla. Fold in the apples and nuts.

Turn into a greased 9″ pie pan and bake 40 minutes in a 350° oven. Serve with hot rum sauce. Makes six to eight servings.

HOT RUM SAUCE:

½ cup butter
½ cup WHITE SUGAR

½ cup BROWN SUGAR
½ cup HALF AND HALF

Mix together all ingredients and boil for one minute. Add 2 tablespoons rum or rum flavoring to taste. Pour hot over each dessert just before serving.

Quick and Easy Apple Pudding

1 EGG
¾ cup SUGAR
½ cup FLOUR
1 tsp. BAKING POWDER
½ tsp. CINNAMON

1 large APPLE, peeled
  cored and diced
¼ cup NUTS (optional)
1 Tbsp. BUTTER (or margarine)

Beat egg, add sugar and beat until lemon-colored. Sift together flour, baking powder and cinnamon, and fold into egg mixture.

Fold in diced apples and nuts. Pour batter into well-greased 8″ pie pan and dot with butter (or margarine). Bake in 350° oven for 25 minutes. Serve plain or with ice cream or whipped cream. Makes six to eight pie-shaped servings.

Apple Tapioca Pudding

½ cup SUGAR
¼ tsp. SALT
2 cups WATER

2 cups peeled, sliced
 APPLES
2 Tbsp. quick-cooking TAPIOCA

Add sugar and salt to water in two-quart saucepan. Place over medium heat and stir until sugar is dissolved. Add apples and cover. Cook slowly until apples are tender, about 15 minutes. Carefully stir in tapioca, continuing to cook until tapioca is transparent.

Serve cold with whipped cream. Makes four servings.

Butterscotch Apple Dessert

2 EGGS
1½ cups SUGAR
3 cups peeled, sliced
 APPLES
1½ cups FLOUR

1½ tsp. BAKING SODA
¾ tsp. ground NUTMEG
¾ tsp. CINNAMON
1 tsp. SALT
1 cup chopped NUTS

Beat eggs well. Add 1½ cups sugar gradually and beat until thick and lemon-colored. Fold in apple slices.

Sift together 1½ cups flour, baking soda, nutmeg, cinnamon and salt. Fold into egg mixture with nuts. Pour batter in greased 13x9x2″ baking pan.

Bake in 325° oven 50-60 minutes or until done. Serve warm with butterscotch sauce. Makes 16 servings.

BUTTERSCOTCH SAUCE

2 Tbsp. FLOUR
¾ cup SUGAR
¾ cup BROWN SUGAR,
 firmly packed

¾ LIGHT CREAM
1/3 cup BUTTER
 (or margarine)

Combine 2 tablespoons flour, ¾ cup sugar and brown sugar in top of double boiler. Stir in cream and butter. Cook over simmering water, stirring occasionally, until thickened.

Danish Apple Cake (Aeblekage)

2 cups fine BREAD CRUMBS
  (or 1 doz. pieces of zwiebach,
  crushed fine)
1/3 cup BUTTER
  (or margarine)

4 cups thick, sweetened
  APPLESAUCE with
1 tsp. VANILLA
½ pt. WHIPPING CREAM
½ cup JELLY (or fruit preserves)

Fry crumbs gently in butter until they are evenly coated and nicely browned. In a glass bowl (about 8″) or other deep dish, place a layer of the buttered crumbs. Over them spread a third of the applesauce, then add two more layers of crumbs and applesauce, finishing with crumbs on the top. Cover and refrigerate overnight.

Before serving add a layer of whipped cream and garnish with bits of jelly, jam or other fruit preserves. Makes 8 to 10 servings.

* *Memo to meal planner: If prepared in a clear glass bowl, this makes a very attractive dessert to serve at the table.*

Apple Cake Dessert

4 cups peeled, sliced
  APPLES
2 cups SUGAR
2 cups FLOUR
1½ tsp. BAKING SODA
1 tsp. SALT

2 tsp. CINNAMON
2 EGGS, beaten
¾ cup SALAD OIL
2 tsp. VANILLA
1 cup chopped NUTS

Mix apples and sugar in large bowl. Let stand a few minutes. Sift together the dry ingredients. Mix with apples. Add eggs, oil, vanilla and nuts. Mix thoroughly. Pour into well greased 9x13″ pan. Bake in 350° oven about 50 minutes. To serve, cut into 12 large or 16 medium-size pieces and top with whipped cream or ice cream.

Blushing Apple Dessert

1/3 cup BUTTER (or margarine)
1 cup FLOUR
1 Tbsp. SUGAR
¾ tsp. BAKING POWDER
¼ tsp. SALT
1 EGG, beaten
1 Tbsp. MILK

6 cups peeled, sliced
  APPLES
1 pkg. (3-oz.) STRAWBERRY
  GELATIN
2 Tbsp. SUGAR
1 cup FLOUR
1 cup SUGAR
½ cup BUTTER (or margarine)

Cream butter until fluffy. Sift together 1 cup flour, 1 tablespoon sugar, baking powder and salt. Combine egg and milk. Add dry ingredients alternately with egg mixture; mix well. Press into 9" spring-form pan. Lay apple slices on dough so they overlap. Combine gelatin and 2 tablespoons sugar; sprinkle over apples.

Combine 1 cup flour and 1 cup sugar. Cut in ½ cup butter (or margarine) until coarse crumbs are formed. Sprinkle crumbs over apples.

Bake in 350° oven 50-60 minutes or until done. Serve with whipped cream, if desired. Makes 12 servings.

Caramel Apple Fondue

Unpeeled APPLE SLICES
  (or chunks)
1 pkg. (14-oz.) CARAMELS

1/3 cup WATER
Chopped NUTS
  (or toasted coconut)

Melt caramels in covered double boiler over simmering water. Add water slowly, blending until smooth. Pour into fondue pot or chafing dish. Keep fondue pot warm. Spear the apple slices, dip them in the caramel and then in nuts.

- *Memo to meal planner:* Instead of using a fondue pot, you may prefer to put the apple slices in individual serving dishes. Top with the caramel mixture and serve with chopped nuts or coconut.

Quick Caramel Apples

6 to 8 WOODEN SKEWERS
6 to 8 medium APPLES

1 pkg. (14-oz.) CARAMELS
3 Tbsp. WATER

Insert skewers in apples. Melt caramels in top of double boiler over simmering water. Add water slowly, blending until smooth. Leaving caramel mixture over hot water, dip apples into caramel mixture. Twirl apples so all sides are covered. Place on waxed paper to cool. (Store in refrigerator if weather is humid.) Makes six to eight servings.

Apple Dumplings

2 cups FLOUR
1 tsp. SALT
2 tsp. BAKING POWDER
¾ cup SHORTENING
3 Tbsp. MILK
8 medium APPLES,
   peeled and cored

SUGAR
CINNAMON
2 cups SUGAR
¼ tsp. CINNAMON
¼ tsp. ground NUTMEG
2 cups hot WATER
¼ cup BUTTER (or margarine)

Sift together flour, salt and baking powder. Cut in shortening until crumbly. Add milk; stir until mixture forms a ball.

Divide dough in half. Roll out on floured surface to 12" square. Cut in four (6") squares. Place 1 apple in the center of each square. Sprinkle each with sugar and cinnamon. Bring corners of dough to top of apple. Pinch edges together. Place in buttered 13x9x2" baking dish. Repeat with remaining dough.

Combine 2 cups sugar, ¼ teaspoon cinnamon and nutmeg in saucepan. Add water and butter (or margarine). Stir over medium heat until sugar is dissolved and butter (or margarine) is melted. Pour syrup around apple dumplings.

Bake in 350° oven 50-60 minutes or until apples are tender. Serve warm with cream. Makes eight servings.

Apple Torte

4 EGGS
½ cup WHITE SUGAR
2/3 cup FLOUR
½ tsp. SALT

1 tsp. BAKING POWDER
1 tsp. VANILLA
2 cups peeled, chopped APPLES
½ to ¾ cup NUTS

Beat eggs till lemon colored, adding sugar as you beat. Combine flour, salt, baking powder and blend into egg mixture. Add vanilla. Fold in the apples and nuts. Turn into 9x9″ pan and bake at 350° for 40-45 minutes. Serve cold with whipped cream or ice cream. Makes 9 to 12 servings.

Frozen Apple Cream

1 cup HEAVY CREAM
¼ cup SUGAR
1½ Tbsp. LEMON JUICE

⅛ tsp. SALT
¾ cup unpeeled, grated
   APPLES

Whip cream until stiff. Fold in sugar, lemon juice, salt and apples. Pour into 9x5x3″ loaf pan. Cover with aluminum foil. Freeze until solid. Spoon into sherbet glasses to serve. Makes six servings.

Apple Ice Cream Sundaes

RED CINNAMON CANDIES
APPLESAUCE

Vanilla ICE CREAM

Dissolve a few cinnamon candies in warm applesauce. Spoon over scoops of vanilla ice cream.

VARIATION: Serve warm applesauce over cinnamon ice cream.

Recipe Notes

Apple Beverages

Hot Spiced Cider

1 qt. APPLE JUICE (or cider)
1 cup WATER
¼ cup BROWN SUGAR,
   firmly-packed

⅛ tsp. SALT
1 stick CINNAMON
6 whole CLOVES

Mix ingredients together and heat, but do not boil. Let stand overnight. Reheat before serving. Makes five cups.

Rosy Glow Apple Cider

2 qts. APPLE JUICE (or cider)
¼ cup RED CINNAMON CANDIES

Heat juice and candies together. Serve hot. Makes eight cups.

Apple Orange Cooler

Chilled APPLE JUICE
Orange SHERBET
Chilled GINGER ALE

Fill punch cups half full with chilled apple juice. Put a spoonful of orange sherbet into each cup and follow with ginger ale, poured in slowly, to make about three-fourths cupful of Cooler.

Holly Berry Punch

2 cups APPLE JUICE, chilled
2 cups CRANBERRY JUICE, chilled

2 cups WATER
1 cup SUGAR
1 qt. GINGER ALE, chilled

Blend apple and cranberry juices together. Dissolve sugar in the water. Add the juices. Just before serving, add the ginger ale. Makes about 25 servings.

- *Memo to meal planner: You can vary this punch by adding one can of orange concentrate with one can of water. To prevent watering down the punch, make the ice mold of fruit juices rather than water.*

Hot Spicy Holiday Punch

2 qts. APPLE JUICE
4 cups CRANBERRY JUICE
2 Tbsp. LEMON JUICE

2 Tbsp. HONEY
2 tsp. whole CLOVES
2 (3-in.) CINNAMON STICKS, broken into pieces

Combine all ingredients. Heat to boiling. Reduce heat and simmer 30 minutes. Taste the punch. If it is too sour, add a little honey. If too sweet, add more lemon juice. If not spicy enough to suit, simmer longer.

Strain and serve hot from a glass pitcher or punch bowl. Makes 3 quarts. Store leftover punch in the refrigerator and reheat as needed.

- *Memo to meal planner: If you serve from a punch bowl, stud an orange or an apple with cloves and float it in the punch.*

Mulled Apple Juice

2 cans (46-oz) APPLE JUICE
1 can (6-oz) frozen LEMONADE
  CONCENTRATE

2 sticks CINNAMON
1 tsp. whole CLOVES
2 or 3 RED APPLES

Combine apple juice and lemonade concentrate in large saucepan. Add cinnamon and cloves, tied in a bag. Heat until juices start to simmer. Remove spice bag. Pour into heat-proof punch bowl. Float two or three red apples which have been studded with additional whole cloves. Serve hot. Makes about 24 servings.

Wassail Bowl

1 can (46-oz) APPLE JUICE
1 can (46-oz) unsweetened
  PINEAPPLE JUICE

1 cup ORANGE JUICE
3 sticks CINNAMON
1 tsp. whole CLOVES

Combine all ingredients in large saucepan. Heat to boiling; reduce heat and simmer 15 to 20 minutes. Remove from heat and strain. Pour hot wassail in heat-proof punch bowl. Garnish with slices of unpeeled apple, studded with cloves, if desired. Makes 24 servings.

Percolator Hot Cider

3 cans (46-oz) APPLE JUICE
1 tsp. whole CLOVES

3 sticks CINNAMON,
  broken in pieces

Pour apple juice in 30-cup electric coffee maker. Put cinnamon and cloves in coffee maker basket. Perk gently as for coffee. Keep hot and serve from the coffee maker. Makes 24 servings.

Cider Sherbet Refresher

2 qts. APPLE JUICE (or cider)
1 qt. lemon SHERBET

1 bottle (10-oz) lemon-lime
 CARBONATED BEVERAGE
Sprigs of MINT

Pour the chilled apple juice over the sherbet which has been spooned into punch bowl. Just before serving, pour the carbonated beverage in gently. Garnish with sprigs of mint. Makes 12 servings.

Spiced Apple Tea

1 can (46-oz) APPLE JUICE
1 Tbsp. HONEY
½ tsp. whole CLOVES

1 CINNAMON STICK,
 broken in pieces
2 TEA BAGS

In saucepan combine apple juice, honey and the spices. Bring to a boil. Remove from heat and add the tea bags. Cover and brew for 3 to 5 minutes. Remove the tea bags. Strain out spices. Serve in mugs. Makes 6 to 8 servings.

Red Apple Wine Punch

½ cup SUGAR
½ cup WATER
1 LEMON, thinly-sliced
1 ORANGE, thinly-sliced
8 whole CLOVES

1 CINNAMON STICK
½ cup ORANGE JUICE
2 cups APPLE JUICE
2 cups Burgundy or
 claret WINE

Mix together sugar, water, lemon and orange slices, cloves and cinnamon. Bring to a boil over low heat and simmer 5 minutes. Add the orange and apple juices and reheat. Add the wine and reheat but do not boil. Strain and serve at once. If you serve from a punch bowl, float the lemon and orange slices in the punch. Makes about 6 cups.

Microwave Recipes

MEMO TO MICROWAVE USERS:

Because microwave ovens vary in their settings and power, you may have to adjust the cooking time suggested in these recipes to your particular oven.

Applesauce

6 to 8 medium APPLES,   ½ cup WATER
  peeled and sliced   ½ cup SUGAR

In a two-quart casserole, combine apples and water. Cover and microwave 8 to 10 minutes on high until apples are soft. Stir once during cooking. Stir in sugar. Let stand. Cover and allow to stand a few minutes. Serves six.

Baked Apples

4 medium-large APPLES   ½ Tbsp. RAISINS
4 Tbsp. BROWN SUGAR   2 Tbsp. BUTTER (or margarine)
¼ tsp. CINNAMON

Wash and core apples. Cut a thin slice of apple off stem end. Make a shallow slit around the circumference of the apple about one inch from the bottom. This keeps the skin from shrinking and helps to retain shape.

Combine brown sugar, cinnamon and raisins. Fill the centers of the apples and place in glass baking dish or individual custard cups.

Cover with waxed paper or vented plastic wrap. Microwave on high 6 to 10 minutes or until tender. Cooking time will depend on size and variety of apple.

Apple Crisp

5 cups APPLES, peeled and sliced
½ cup FLOUR
¾ cup quick-cooking OATMEAL
½ cup BROWN SUGAR, firmly packed
½ tsp. CINNAMON
½ cup BUTTER (or margarine)

Arrange apples in a two-quart 8x8" glass baking dish. Combine flour, oatmeal, brown sugar and cinnamon. Cut in butter (or margarine) until crumbly. Sprinkle over apples. Microwave 12 to 15 minutes on high until apples are tender. Makes six servings.

Microwave Apple Pie

Preheat conventional oven to 425°.

Prepare your favorite two-crust apple pie or use the apple pie recipes in this book.

Use a nine-inch glass pie plate.

Slit the top crust, making a generous slit in the center.

Microwave on high 10 minutes or until juices start bubbling through slits. The crust will not brown.

Place the pie in the preheated (425°) conventional oven and bake 8 to 10 minutes or until crust is golden brown.

Cool on a wire rack.

Preserving Apples

- Making Apple Jelly, Jam and Other Preserves
- Apple Jelly Recipes
- Recipes for Jam, Conserve, Butter, Pickles & Chutney
- Canning Apples
- Making Applesauce
- Applesauce Recipes
- Freezing Apples & Applesauce
- Freezing Apple Pies
- Drying Apples

Preserving Apples

It happens every other year in your backyard. Your apple trees are loaded with beautiful fruit. Of course you're delighted, but how can you use all those apples—not let any go to waste? You give some to the neighbors, the family eats them fresh every day, you bake pies, cakes, cobblers, crisps—until the family exclaims, "Not another apple dessert!"

There are many other possibilities for using apples—the versatility of this fruit is amazing. You may want to declare a moratorium on apple desserts, but not on applesauce. Keep some in the refrigerator to spoon over pancakes or French toast, or flavor it to serve with meats (see Applesauce recipes).

To preserve apple goodness for winter use, make that spicy Pennsylvania Dutch favorite, apple butter. Or try our recipe for apple jellies, pickles and chutney. Can some applesauce, too; and freeze apples for pie—or freeze the pies, already baked.

Should you make apple juice or cider from your surplus apples? It's possible, certainly, but it's a complicated process—and you'd probably be happier buying it commercially produced. Recipes for apple preserves and applesauce follow.

Making Apple Jelly, Jam and Other Preserves

The secret to success in jelly making is to prepare small amounts: about 4 cups juice at one time. NEVER double the recipe!

Wash jars and rinse well in hot water or run through the dishwasher. Sterilize jars and keep jars hot in hot water until you are ready to use them, so they won't break when filled with the hot jelly or jam.

Carefully wash apples and crabapples. Remove any bruised part. Do not use decayed fruit. Follow recipe to make jam, jelly or preserves. Pack in hot sterilized jars. Leave ⅛-inch head space. Wipe sealing edge of jar. Add lid and adjust ring. Sterilize in boiling water for five minutes. Remove jars from canner. Cool on a rack. Test for seals, label, date and store in a cool, dry place.

Easy Apple Jelly

4 cups APPLE JUICE
(commercially canned)

5 cups SUGAR
1 pkg. powdered PECTIN

Measure juice into large saucepan. Mix pectin with the juice and bring to a hard boil. Immediately add the sugar and stir. Bring back to full boil again and boil one minute, stirring constantly. Remove from the heat and skim off foam. Pour into hot, sterilized jars and process in a hot water bath five minutes. Makes about six (8-oz.) jars.

- *Memo to meal planner: Adding a few drops of red food coloring will give the jelly a lovely color.*

Apple Jelly

3 lbs. tart APPLES
3 cups WATER

2 Tbsp. LEMON JUICE
3 cups SUGAR

Choose tart apples, ¾ of them fully ripe and ¼ under-ripe. Wash, remove stem and blossom end. Do not peel or core. Cut apples into small pieces. Place apples and water in saucepan. Cover and bring to a boil over high heat. Reduce heat and simmer 10 to 25 minutes or until apples are soft.

Place fruit in colander lined with cheesecloth or in a dampened jelly bag. Let fruit drip through without pressing so jelly will be clear. However, you will get more juice by pressing and/or twisting bag or using a fruit press.

Measure apple juice into kettle. Add lemon juice and sugar. Stir well. Bring to a boil over high heat until temperature is 220° or jelly mixture sheets from spoon. Remove from heat. Skim off foam quickly. Pour jelly immediately into hot, sterilized jars, leaving ⅛" headspace. Process in hot water bath five minutes. Makes about five (6-oz.) jars.

Crabapple Jelly

3 lbs. CRABAPPLES
3 cups WATER

3 cups SUGAR

Follow directions for making Apple Jelly, except omit the lemon juice. Makes five (6-oz.) jars.

Mint Jelly

6 cups APPLE JUICE
4 cups SUGAR

½ tsp. PEPPERMINT EXTRACT
GREEN COLORING

Measure apple juice into kettle. Add sugar. Stir well. Bring to a boil over high heat until temperature is 220° or until jelly mixture sheets from spoon. Remove from heat. Skim off foam quickly. Add peppermint extract and enough green coloring to tint jelly delicately. Pour into hot sterilized jars, leaving ⅛-inch headspace. Wipe top of jars with clean, damp cloth. Dip covers in hot water and place on jars. Put on screw bands and screw firmly into place. Process in hot water bath five minutes. Makes six (6-oz.) jars.

Apple Peach Jam

4 cups peeled, chopped
  APPLES
4 cups peeled, chopped
  PEACHES

1 Tbsp. grated LEMON RIND
½ cup LEMON JUICE
7 cups SUGAR

Combine apples, peaches, lemon rind, lemon juice and sugar. Cook slowly until thick and transparent, stirring frequently. Ladle into sterilized jars; adjust lids and process in boiling water bath for five minutes. Makes four pints.

Apple Conserve

4½ cups unpeeled, finely
  chopped tart APPLES
½ cup WATER
¼ cup LEMON JUICE

½ cup RAISINS
1 pkg. powdered FRUIT PECTIN
5 cups SUGAR
½ cup chopped WALNUTS

Combine apples, water, lemon juice and raisins in kettle. Add fruit pectin; stir well. Place over high heat and bring to a full boil. Stirring constantly, stir in sugar. Bring to a full boil again. Boil one minute, stirring constantly. Stir in nuts. Remove from heat. Skim and stir five minutes. Ladle into hot, sterilized jars to within ½-inch from top. Adjust jar lids. Process in boiling water bath 10 minutes. Makes five half-pints.

Apple Butter

6 lbs. APPLES,
  quartered and cored
2 qts. APPLE JUICE

3 cups SUGAR
1½ tsp. CINNAMON
½ tsp. ground CLOVES

Combine apples and apple juice in saucepan. Cook until apples are tender. Put through a food mill. Place 12 cups apple pulp into kettle. Cook pulp until thick enough to round up in spoon. Stir pulp frequently as it thickens to prevent sticking. Add sugar, cinnamon and cloves; continue cooking slowly until mixture is thick, about one hour. Pour into hot, sterilized jars to within ¼-inch from top. Adjust jar lids. Process in boiling water bath 10 minutes. Makes six pints.

Crabapple Pickles

3 qts. CRABAPPLES
2 cups VINEGAR
4 cups SUGAR

2 cups WATER
2 sticks CINNAMON
1 tsp. whole CLOVES

Wash crabapples using only ones free from blemishes. Combine vinegar, sugar and water in kettle. Bring to a boil. Tie cinnamon and cloves in cheesecloth; add to mixture. Boil for 10 minutes. Add crabapples to syrup. Cook until almost tender. Place crabapples in hot, sterilized jars. Pour hot syrup over crabapples to within ½-inch from top. Adjust jar lids. Process in boiling hot water bath 10 minutes. Makes six pints.

Anna's and Esther's Apple Chutney

4 cups chopped, peeled
  APPLES
½ cup WATER
3 cups SUGAR

¼ cup VINEGAR
1 tsp. CINNAMON
¼ tsp. ground CLOVES
¼ tsp. SALT

Place apples and water in a two-quart saucepan. Bring to a boil. Cover and simmer 10 minutes or until apples are tender. Stir in sugar, vinegar, cinnamon, cloves and salt. Simmer, uncovered, 50 minutes or until mixture thickens. Pour into hot, sterilized jars to within one-half inch from top. Adjust jar lids. Process in boiling water bath 10 minutes. Makes four half-pints.

Canning Apples

Check the apple chart, "Know Your Apples," to see what varieties are best for pie and sauce, or use your backyard apples.

Canned apples will keep without sugar, though most fruits have better color, flavor and texture when canned with sugar or a sugar syrup.

To can applesauce...

make the sauce your usual way or use our recipe. Sweeten it or not, as you wish, and pack hot in hot jars to ¼-inch of the top. Process pints and quarts for 25 minutes in a boiling water bath.

To can apples for pie...

peel, core and cut apples into pieces or slices. To prevent darkening, drop cut apples into a solution of 1 gallon water to 2 tablespoons each salt and vinegar. Do not soak more than 15 minutes. Drain, then boil for 5 minutes in water or in a thin sugar syrup (recipe follows). This will help apples hold their shape better.

Pack apples in hot jars. Cover with hot thin sugar syrup to ½-inch of jar top. Process in boiling water bath, pints 15 minutes and quarts 20 minutes.

To make thin sugar syrup, combine 2 cups sugar and 4 cups water. Bring to a boil; boil 5 minutes. Skim if necessary. Makes 5 cups.

To use canned apples in pie...

drain them and mix with spices, adding sugar if needed. How much sugar depends on sweetness or tartness of apples and your family's preference.

Making Applesauce

Smooth Applesauce: Small Quantity

4 medium APPLES
½ cup WATER

¼ cup SUGAR

Peel, quarter and core apples. Place apples and water in saucepan. Cover and simmer 10 minutes or until apples are very tender, stirring occasionally to prevent scorching. For a smooth applesauce, put apples through a food mill. Stir in sugar. Makes about two cups.

Chunky Applesauce: Small Quantity

Cook as above. Break up the cooked apples slightly with a fork.

Smooth Applesauce: Large Quantity

Peel, quarter and core apples. Place in a large kettle with enough water so fruit will not stick to bottom during cooking. Stir occasionally to prevent scorching. Cover and simmer 10 minutes or until apples are tender. For very smooth sauce, put through food mill.

One bushel of apples will yield 16 to 20 quarts of applesauce.

Slick Tricks for Applesauce

Relish for Meats—Use applesauce as is or:
Sweeten with cinnamon candies and serve hot or cold with pork.

Mix with horseradish to suit your taste—a generous amount to give some "bite" or a small amount to impart a subtle flavor. Serve with beef, ham or pork.

Toppings—Use unsweetened applesauce on:
- Hot gingerbread instead of whipped cream
- French toast
- Pancakes and waffles
- Cinnamon ice cream or vanilla

Quickie Desserts
See recipe for Apple-Graham Cracker Delight under *Desserts*.

Freezing Apples & Applesauce

Freezing tends to soften apple texture, so use firm-fleshed cooking varieties suitable for pie (see chart), and freeze them shortly after harvesting. Apples that have been in storage for long periods may darken more quickly after freezing. Frozen apples may be stored one year or longer at 0°F.

Three methods of freezing apples:
1. Peel apples, core and cut into pie slices. An ascorbic acid powder sold in supermarkets to prevent browning of fruit may be used. Follow package directions. Fill container, seal, label, date and freeze.
2. Peel and slice apples; soak in a weak brine solution for 15

minutes (½ cup salt to 1 gallon water). Drain and pack in freezer containers. Cover with sugar syrup: 2 cups sugar and ½ teaspoon crystalline ascorbic acid dissolved in 1 quart cold water. The ascorbic acid helps keep apples from darkening. Seal, label, date, freeze.

3. If apples are in perfect condition and if you have room in your freezer, you can freeze apples whole. Wash but do not peel; pack 6-8 apples in a plastic bag. Label, date and freeze.

To use frozen apples...

do not thaw. Run cold water over each apple and peel while still frozen; use immediately for pie or other cooked desserts. These apples will darken quickly if you thaw them.

To use frozen apple slices in pie...

partially thaw and drain. Sweeten with ¼ to ½-cup sugar, depending on sweetness or tartness of apples. Mix the sugar with spices and a little flour or other thickener, even if you don't usually thicken your fresh apple pies. Frozen apples are more juicy than fresh apples and you must compensate for this.

To freeze applesauce...

sweeten it to taste after cooking or use your favorite applesauce recipe; cool and pack in containers to within ¾-inch of top. Seal, label, date and freeze.

Freezing Apple Pies

One of the most satisfying ways to preserve your surplus apples is in pie crust. It's great to have baked apple pies in your freezer, ready to serve when company drops in unexpectedly. Laboratory tests at the University of Minnesota show that baked pies freeze more satisfactorily than unbaked pies. You can keep a baked pie up to six months in your freezer, but use an unbaked pie within three months.

Prepare pies as usual. (See recipes in this book.) Cool baked pies rapidly; then place in the freezer unwrapped. Keep pie level while it is freezing. When frozen, wrap, label, date and return to freezer for storage. (Both baked and unbaked pies freeze faster when unwrapped, and they're easier to wrap after they're frozen.)

To serve a baked frozen apple pie...

let it stand at room temperature for 20-30 minutes; then place on the lower shelf of a preheated 350° F. oven and heat until warm, about 30 minutes. If your pie pan is shiny light-weight aluminum, place on cookie sheet in the oven.

To bake a frozen unbaked pie...

place it on the lower shelf of a preheated 450°F. oven. Bake for 10-15 minutes; then reduce heat to 400°F. Total baking time will be 10-20 minutes longer than regular baking time as specified in recipe.

Drying Apples

Drying is one of the oldest methods of food preservation. Today, it's done under considerably more hygienic conditions than those described in Chapter I.

If you have your own dehydrator, follow manufacturer's directions. Otherwise, directions are given below.

Use varieties of good dessert or cooking quality, mature but not soft. Wash, peel and core apples and cut into slices or rings ⅛ to ¼-inch thick. To prevent browning, dip in a solution of 1 cup water and 2½ teaspoons pure ascorbic acid, or steam-blanch 10 minutes. Spread the slices on trays no more than two layers deep. Under controlled heat it will take approximately six hours to dry the apple slices in the oven (about two hours at each temperature level). Start the oven at 130° and gradually increase the heat to 165°, finishing at 145°. If you do not have much control over your oven or dryer, try to keep the temperature at 140° to 145° for approximately six hours. For an evenly dried product, the slices must be stirred occasionally. The finished, dried product should be leathery and suede-like without any moisture when cut or squeezed.

You can dry apple slices in the sun if you have a few days of hot, dry, breezy weather, but it is difficult to maintain hygienic conditions when sun-drying. Sun-drying may take several days, and you should be prepared to finish drying indoors if weather conditions change. Once started, drying should be continuous until enough moisture is removed to keep the fruit from spoiling.

For more detailed directions on drying procedures and equipment, check with the Agricultural Extension Service in your state.

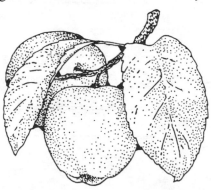

Recipe Notes

Fun with Apples

- Pomander Balls
- Apple Centerpiece
- Apple Candle Holders
- Party Favors
- Santa Claus Favors
- Bobbing for Apples
- Apple on a String
- Apple Peel Fortunes
- Apple Puppet Contest
- Apple Race
- Apple Seed Guessing Game

Fun with Apples

Every kid bobs for apples at Halloween, but have you ever run an apple race? Or tried making apple head dolls? Or apple candle holders? Or pomanders, for gifts or to perfume your own closets? Here are some suggestions for several ways to have fun with apples.

Pomander Balls

Originally, pomanders were apple-shaped mixtures of aromatic substances, which people carried as protection against infection. Now, we enjoy them for the pleasant way they scent our closets.

For each ball, you need an apple, a box of whole cloves, a pipe cleaner and ribbon. Poke holes all over the apple with a sharp-pointed round toothpick and insert cloves. Cloves should be close together, completely covering the apple. Insert a pipe cleaner into the stem end—be sure it's secure. Bend it to make a hanger, and decorate with a ribbon bow. The apple will dry, but the spicy fragrance will remain.

Apple Centerpiece

Select the reddest, most attractive apples you can find. Wash and polish them until they shine. Pile them on a tray with sprigs of evergreen. For a Christmas table, set some miniature Santa figures climbing over the greens—or the Scandinavian *nisse* or *tomte*. For an autumn table, use yellow apples like Golden Delicious or Honey Gold, and arrange some of fall's bright colored leaves among the greens.

Apple Candle Holders

Select firm, well-shaped red apples. Polish highly. Remove the core from the stem end with an apple corer, leaving about ½-inch of fruit at the base. Insert candles.

Party Favors

Use apples as flag holders. For an international party, put an apple with the flag of a different nation at each place at the table. If you're entertaining after a football game, make college banners of construction paper in the appropriate colors. Glue them to thin wood picks and insert in apples.

Santa Claus Favors

For each apple Santa, you'll need a large red apple, five large marshmallows, six large round red gumdrops, four whole cloves, three cinnamon candies (red hots) and round toothpicks. Make legs and arms by threading a marshmallow and a gumdrop on a toothpick; insert in apple with gumdrop next to apple (marshmallow makes "fur" cuffs). Make the head the same way, adding a gumdrop hat. Press red hots into marshmallow head for eyes and nose. Stick cloves into apple body for buttons. If you wish, add beard and pompon of cotton.

Bobbing for Apples

Here's the favorite game for Halloween parties. To play it, fill a washtub, baby's bathtub or large plastic vessel three-quarters full of water. Count a few more apples than there are players. Float the apples in the water. The idea is for players to catch an apple with their teeth—without using hands—and within a certain time limit. The person who gets his apple out of the water first is the winner, but others continue to try until time is called.

Apple on a String

Another favorite Halloween contest. Each player—with his hands behind him—tries to eat an apple dangling from a string in a doorway or some open place. To make the game more interesting, hang the apples at different heights.

Apple Peel Fortunes

Write out fortunes that will be appropriate for the guests you've invited. Turn them over and number the other side; arrange them, number-side-up, on the floor. Ask each guest to peel an apple and toss the peeling over his or her shoulder. The fortune nearest where the peeling falls will be his to read aloud.

Apple Puppet Contest

Divide the group into teams. Give each team several apples, an apple corer, knife, and pins, and have available a large box of articles that can be used for clothing the puppets—scarves, doll hats and dresses, ribbons, feathers, jewelry, etc. Each team decides on a fairy tale or Mother Goose rhyme to enact. Players then carve appropriate apple puppets, coring the apples o fit players' index fingers. Puppet faces are carved much like a jack-o'lantern, and painted, if desired, with lipstick or crayons. Stage can be a table covered with a cloth to hide the puppeteers.

Apple Race

This game can be very funny. Divide the group into teams. Give each player a toothpick. Object is to push an apple along from starting point to goal using only the toothpick held in the mouth—no hands. The side that gets all its apples to the goal first wins.

Apple Seed Guessing Game

Show guests a shiny red apple and ask each one to write down the number of seeds in the apple. Collect the answers; then cut the apple and let everyone help count seeds. Give a prize to the person whose guess is closest.

Index

A

Aeblekage, 88
Appetizers, 33-34
  Apple Appetizers 34
  Apple Appetizers,
    Cookout, 34
  Apple Dip, 33
  Apple Spread, 33
  Cheddar Dip, 34
  Creamy Apple Dip, 33
Apple(s)
  Amber, 81
  Apricot Loaf, 46
  Baked, 81, 97
  Bars, 53-58
  Batter Pudding, 85
  Blueberry Bread, 46
  Blueberry Cake, 69
  Blueberry Pie, 72
  Blushing Dessert, 89
  Butter, 103
  Butternut Bake, 42
  Butterscotch Dessert, 87
  Cakes, 59-70
  Caramel, Quick, 90
  Cereal Cookies, 56
  Charts (varieties), 20-24
  Cheese Crisp, 83, 98
  Cheese Dessert, Creamy, 82
  Cheese Salad, 38
  Cheese Sandwich Bread, 47
  Chutney, 103
  Cider, 93, 95
  Cinnamon Salad, 37
  Cinnamon Waffles, 49
  Coconut Dessert, 82
  Coffee Cake, Quick, 60
  Conserve, 102
  Crab Meat Salad, 40
  Cranberry Crisp, 83
  Cranberry Pie, 78
  Cranberry Relish Pie, 77
  Cream, Frozen, 91
  Cream Pie, 74
  Crisp, 83, 98
  Crumb Pie with Yogurt, 75
  Danish Pastry Squares, 73
  Dip, 33
  Doughnut Balls, 52
  Doughnuts, 52
  Dream Bars, 54
  Dumplings, 90
  Finnish Sugar Cake, 66
  French Pie, 74

  Fruit Salad, Blushing, 37
  Gourmet Pie, 76
  Graham Cracker
    Delight, 84
  Honey Buns, 48
  Ice Cream Pie, 73
  Ice Cream Sundaes, 91
  Jelly, 101
  Juice, Mulled, 95
  Lemon Sauce Cake, 68
  Macaroon Dessert, 84
  Muffins, 50
  Nut Bars, 57
  Oat Bran Muffins, 51
  Oatmeal Bars, 53
  Oatmeal Crunch, 84
  Old-Fashioned Pie, 72
  Orange Cooler, 93
  Orange Cranberry
    Salad, 40
  Pancakes, 49
  Peach Jam, 102
  Pear Crumb Pie, 75
  Pecan Kuchen, 47
  Pecan Pie,
    Upside Down, 79
  Pizza Pie, 77
  Pudding Dessert, 85
  Pudding Pie, 86
  Pumpkin Pie, 79
  Raisin Bread, 45
  Raisin Pie, 78
  Sour Cream Pie, 76
  Spread, 33
  Squares, Danish, 73
  Streusel Coffee Cake, 61
  Streusel Muffins, 50
  Stuffing, 43
  Tapioca Pudding, 87
  Torte, 91
  Upside Down Cake, 64
  Walnut Brownics, 58
  Whole Wheat Cake, 69
Applesauce, 104-106
  Cake with Apple Juice, 66
  Frosting, 66
  Canning, 104
  Chocolate Cup Cakes, 62
  Chunky, 105
  Date Cake, 63
  Date-Nut Cookies, 57
  Freezing, 105-106
  Honey Rolls, 51
  Apple Appetizers, 34
  Large Quantity, 105

  Lime Mold, 39
  Orange Bars, 53
  Pecan Rolls, 45
  Puffs, 48
  Smooth, 04, 105
  Tricks, 105
Appleseed, Johnny, 7-8
  (John Chapman)
Apricot Apple Loaf, 46
Ascorbic acid, 106
Autumn Coffee Cake, 59

B

Baked Apples, 81, 97
Baldwin (variety), 16, 22
Bars, 53-58
  Apple Dream, 54
  Apple Nut, 57
  Apple Oatmeal, 53
  Apple Walnut Brownies, 58
  Applesauce Orange, 53
  Spicy Apple Squares, 55
Beacon (variety), 17
Beecher, Rev. Henry Ward, 11
Beverages, 93-96
  Apple Orange Cooler, 93
  Cider Sherbet Refresher, 96
  Holly Berry Punch, 94
  Hot Spiced Cider, 93
  Hot Spicy Holiday
    Punch, 94
  Mulled Apple Juice, 95
  Percolator Hot Cider, 95
  Red Apple Wine Punch, 96
  Rosy Glow Cider, 93
  Spiced Apple Tea, 96
  Wassail Bowl, 95
Blueberry
  Apple Bread, 46
  Apple Cake, 69
  Apple Pie, 72
Blushing Apple Dessert, 89
Blushing Apple Fruit
  Salad, 37
Brandy, 10
Breads, 45-52
  Apple Apricot Loaf, 46
  Apple Blueberry, 46
  Apple Cheese Sandwich, 47
  Apple Cinnamon
    Waffles, 49
  Apple Doughnut Balls, 52
  Apple Doughnuts, 52
  Apple Honey Buns, 48

Breads (continued)
  Apple Muffins, 50
  Apple Pancakes, 49
  Apple Pecan Kuchen, 47
  Apple-Raisin Bread, 45
  Apple Streusel Muffins, 50
  Applesauce Honey
    Rolls, 51
  Applesauce Pecan Rolls, 45
  Applesauce Puffs, 48
Brownies, 58
Budding, 14
Buns, 48
Butterscotch Apple Desert, 87

C

CA (Controlled Atmosphere
  Storage), 19
Cakes, 59-70
  Apple Blueberry, 69
  Apple Lemon Sauce, 68
  Apple Streusel, 61
  Apple Upside Down, 64
  Apple Whole Wheat, 69
  Applesauce, 66
  Applesauce Chocolate
    Cupcakes, 62
  Applesauce Date, 63
  Autumn Apple, 59
  Cocoa Apple, 67
  Dixie's Fresh Apple, 62
  Easy Apple Spice, 70
  Em's Eggless Applesauce
    Fruit, 67
  Finnish Apple Sugar, 66
  Fresh Fruit, 70
  Ginger Upside Down, 64
  Quick Apple, 60
  Rosy Apple, 65
  Simple Simon, 61
  Sour Cream Apple, 65
  Spicy Apple, 60
Calories in apples, 29
Canning apples, 104
Canning applesauce, 104
Caramel Apple Fondue, 89
Caramel Apples, 90
Centennial crabapple
  (variety), 24
Cereal Apple Cookies, 56
Chapman, John (Johnny
  Appleseed), 7-8
Cheese
  Apple Cheese Salad, 38
  Apple Crisp, 83, 98
  Apple Dip, 33
  Apple Sandwich Bread, 47

Apple Spread, 33
  Cheddar Dip, 34
  Creamy Apple Cheese, 82
  Creamy Apple Dip, 33
Chestnut crabapple
  (variety), 24
Chicken Salad, 38
Chocolate Applesauce
  Cupcakes, 62
Chutney, Apple, 103
Cider
  Hot Spiced, 93
  Percolator Hot, 95
  Rosy Glow Apple, 93
  Sherbet Refresher, 96
Cinnamon Apple Salad, 37
Cocoa Apple Cake, 67
Coconut Apple Dessert, 82
Coffee Cake, 59-61
  Apple Streusel, 61
  Autumn Apple, 59
  Quick Apple, 60
  Spicy Apple, 60
Coleslaw Apple Salad, 37
Connell Red (variety), 22
Conserve, Apple, 102
Cookies, 54-57
  Apple Cereal, 56
  Apple Chip, 54
  Apple Chip Oatmeal, 56
  Applesauce Date Nut, 57
  Oatmeal Apple-Raisin, 55
Cortland (variety), 20
Crabapple(s)
  Chart, 24
  Jelly, 101
  Pickles, 103
Cranberry
  Apple Crisp, 83
  Apple Pie, 78
  Apple Salad, 39
  Relish Apple Pie, 77
Creamy Apple Cheese, 82
Creamy Apple Dip, 33
Crevecoeur, St. John de, 9
Crimson Beauty (variety), 17
Crispin, 22
Cup Cakes, 62

D

Danish Apple Cake
  (Aeblekage), 88
Danish Pastry Squares, 73
Date Applesauce Cake, 63
Date Nut Applesauce
  Cookies, 57

Delicious, Early
  (variety), 17, 20
Delicious, Golden
  (variety), 16, 20
Delicious, Red
  (variety), 16, 20
Desserts, 81-91
  Amber Apples, 81
  Apple Batter Pudding, 85
  Apple Cake Dessert, 88
  Apple Cheese Crisp, 83
  Apple Coconut, 82
  Apple Cranberry Crisp, 83
  Apple Crisp, 83
  Apple Dumplings, 90
  Apple Graham Cracker
    Delight, 84
  Apple Ice Cream
    Sundaes, 91
  Apple Macaroon
    Dessert, 84
  Apple Pudding Dessert, 85
  Apple Pudding Pie, 86
  Apple Tapioca Pudding, 87
  Apple Torte, 91
  Baked Apples, 81
  Blushing Apple Dessert, 89
  Butterscotch Apple
    Dessert, 87
  Caramel Apple Fondue, 89
  Creamy Apple Cheese, 82
  Danish Apple Cake
    (Aeblekage), 88
  Danish Pastry Squares, 73
  Frozen Apple Cream, 91
  Oatmeal Apple Crunch, 84
  Quick Easy Apple
    Pudding, 86
  Quick Caramel Apples, 90
Dolgo crabapple (variety), 24
Doughnuts, Apple Ball, 52
Drying apples, 9, 107
Duchess (variety), 17
Dumplings, Apple, 90
Dwarf apple trees, 14

E-F

Early Delicious (variety), 17
Early McIntosh (variety), 17
Easy Apple Spice Cake, 70
Easy Apple Jelly, 101
Empire (variety), 20
English Pippin (variety), 16
Eggless Applesauce
  Fruit Cake, 67
Fenton (variety), 17

Festive Red and
    White Salad, 36
Finnish Apple Sugar Cake, 66
Fireside (variety), 22
Fort Vancouver, 11
Freezing apples, 105-106
Freezing apple pies, 106-107
Freezing applesauce, 105-106
French Apple Pie, 74
Fresh Fruit Cake, 70
Frosting, 66
Frozen Apple Cream, 91
Fruit Cake, 67, 70
Fruit Salad, 37
Fruited Cranberry
    Apple Salad, 39
Fuji (variety), 20

G-K

Gala (variety), 20
Gideon, Peter, 16-17
Ginger Upside Down Cake, 64
Glossy Raisin Pie, 78
Golden Delicious
    (variety), 15-16, 20
Golden Reinette (variety), 16
Golden Salad, 35
Gourmet Pie, 76
Grafting, 14-15
Granny Smith (variety), 22
Gravenstein (variety), 17
Greeley, Horace, 9
Greening, Northwestern, 21
Grimes Golden (variety), 21
Haralson (variety), 21
Hiatt, Jesse, 16
Holly-Berry Punch, 94
Honey Apple Buns, 48
Honey Applesauce Rolls, 51
Ice Cream Pie, 73
Ice Cream Sundaes, 91
Idared (variety), 21
Jam, Peach, 102
Jelly, Apple, 101
Jelly, Crabapple, 101
Jelly, Mint, 102
Jonagold (variety), 22
Jonathan (variety), 21
Kuchen, Apple Pecan, 47

L-M

Lemon Sauce Apple Cake, 68
Lime Applesauce Mold, 39
Lodi (variety), 17

Main Dishes and
    Side Dishes, 41-44
    Apple Butternut Bake, 42
    Apple Stuffing, 43
    Meatballs & Apple
        Sauerkraut, 41
    Pork Chops and Apples, 41
    Puffy Apple Omelet, 43
    Sweet Potato Apple
        Casserole, 42
McIntosh (variety), 16, 21
McIntosh, Early (variety), 17
McIntosh, John, 16
Mantet (variety), 17
Meatballs/Sauerkraut, 41
Melba (variety), 17
Microwave, 97-98
    Apple Crisp, 98
    Apple Pie, 98
    Applesauce, 97
    Baked Apples, 97
Miller Red (variety), 17
Mint Jelly, 102
Muffins
    Apple, 50
    Apple Oat Bran, 51
    Applesauce Puffs, 48
    Apple Streusel, 50
Mulled Apple Juice, 95
Mullens, Anderson, 15
Mutsu (variety), 22

N-O

Northern Spy (variety), 22
Northwestern Greening
    (variety), 21
Nutrients, 29
Oat Bran Muffins, 51
Oatmeal
    Apple Chip Cookies, 56
    Apple Crunch, 84
    Apple-Raisin Cookies, 55
Oldenburg (variety), 17
Old-fashioned Apple Pie, 72
Orchardists' work, 25-28
Orchards, local, 17
Oriole (variety), 17

P

Pancakes, Apple, 49
Pastry (see also Pies), 71-79
    for 1-crust 8" to 9" pie, 71
    for 2-crust 9" pie, 71

Paula Red (variety), 17-18
Pear Apple Crumb Pie, 75
Pecan Apple Kuchen, 47
Pecan Apple Upside
    Down Pie, 79
Pennsylvania Dutch, 10
Percolator Hot Cider, 95
Picking Apples, 25-28
Pickles, Crabapples, 103
Pies, 71-79
    Apple Blueberry, 72
    Apple Cranberry Relish, 77
    Apple Cream, 74
    Apple Crumb, with
        Yogurt, 75
    Apple Ice Cream, 73
    Apple Pear Crumb, 75
    Apple Pizza, 77
    Apple Pumpkin, 79
    Canned Apples, 104
    Cranberry Apple, 78
    Danish Pastry Squares, 73
    Freezing directions, 106
    French Apple, 74
    Frozen Apples, 101
    Glossy Apple Raisin, 78
    Gourmet Apple, 76
    Ice Cream, 73
    Old-fashioned Apple, 72
    Pizza Apple, 77
    Sour Cream Apple, 76
    Upside Down Apple
        Pecan, 79
Pizza Pie, 77
Pollination, 25-28
Pork Chops and Apples, 41
Preserves
    Apple Butter, 103
    Apple Chutney, 103
    Apple Conserve, 102
    Apple Jelly, 101
    Apple Mint Jelly, 102
    Apple Peach Jam, 102
    Applesauce, 104-106
    Crabapple Jelly, 101
    Crabapple Pickles, 103
    Easy Apple Jelly, 101
Preserving, 99-107
Pruning, 25-28
Pudding, Apple Tapioca, 87
Puffy Apple Omelet, 43
Pumpkin Apple Pie, 79
Punch, 94-96
    Holly Berry, 94
    Hot Spicy Holiday, 94
    Red Apple Wine, 96
    Wassail Bowl, 95

Q-R

Quality (judging), 18
Quick Apple Coffee Cake, 60
Quick Caramel Apples, 90
Quick & Easy Apple
 Pudding, 86
Raisin Apple Pie, 78
Red Apple Wine Punch, 96
Red Delicious (variety), 16, 20
Rhode Island Greening
 (variety), 21
Rob Rob (variety), 17
Rolls, 45, 48, 51
 Apple Honey Buns, 48
 Applesauce Honey, 51
 Applesauce Pecan, 45
Rome Beauty (variety), 21
Rosy Apple Cake, 65

S

Salads, 35-40
 Apple Cheese, 38
 Apple-Crab Meat, 40
 Apple-Orange Cranberry, 40
 Blushing Apple Fruit, 37
 Chicken, 38
 Cinnamon Apple, 37
 Coleslaw Apple, 37
 Festive Red and
  White, 36
 Fruited Cranberry-
  Apple, 39
 Golden, 35
 Lime Applesauce Mold, 39
 Tuna-Apple, 35
 Waldorf, 35
 Waldorf, Oriental, 36
Scion, 14
Seedlings, 14
Shipping, 11-12
Side dishes, 41-44
Simple Simon Cake, 61
Sour Cream Apple Cake, 65
Sour Cream Apple Pie, 76
Spartan (variety), 21
Spraying, 25-28
Squares, Danish Pastry, 73
Squares, Spicy Apple, 60
Stark Brothers Nursery, 15
Stark, C. M., 15
Stayman (variety), 23
Storage, 18-19
Sugar Syrup, Thin, 104
Summer Champion
 (variety), 17
Summer Red (variety), 17
Sundaes, Apple Ice Cream, 91
Sweet Potato Apple
 Casserole, 42

T

Tea, Spiced Apple, 96
Thinning, 25-28
Thin Sugar Syrup, 104
Torte, Apple, 91
Tuna-Apple Salad, 35
Tydeman's Red (variety), 17

U-Z

U.S. apple production, 12
U.S. Grade labels, 18
Upside Down
 Apple Cake, 64
 Apple Pecan Pie, 79
 Ginger Apple Cake, 64
Vancouver, 11-12
Varieties
 apple charts, 20-24
 breeding, 14
 crabapples, 6-7, 24
 late summer/early fall, 17
 late fall, 17, 22-23
 mid-fall, 17, 20-21
 production, 12
 uses of, 17-18, 20-24
Vitamins, 29
Waffles, Apple Cinnamon, 49
Waldorf Salad, 35
Waldorf Oriental Salad, 36
Washington state, 11-12, 15
Wassail Bowl, 95
Wealthy (variety), 17
Wellington (variety), 17
Whitney crabapple (variety), 24
William's Red (variety), 17
Winesap (variety), 23
Yellow Newton (variety), 23
Yellow Transparent
 (variety), 17
York Imperial (variety), 23

Meet the Authors!

Shirley Munson is an associate professor at the University of Minnesota, Department of Horticultural Science, in charge of the Sensory and Food Quality Evaluation Laboratory where apples (and other fruits and vegetables) are evaluated for color, texture, flavor-aroma, keeping and cooking qualities.

For about 15 years, she and her staff set up apple displays and apple dishes at the Minnesota State Fair. Many of her best recipes from these 15 years of exhibits are now included in the *Apple-Lovers' Cook Book*.

Professor Munson is the author of numerous research papers and extension publications on apples, small fruits and vegetables.

She is a recognized authority on home freezing and has several publications on the subject. She has served as a consultant to the freezer manufacturing industry.

A member of a number of professional organizations, Prof. Munson holds BS and MS degrees from the University of Minnesota, College of Home Economics. She enjoys golfing, swimming, skiing and gardening—even growing a few backyard apple trees!

Jo Nelson is the author of a book popular with young people, *Looking Forward to a Career in Home Economics.*

As a freelancer, she has had numerous articles published in national journals and magazines. Appropriately, and perhaps prophetically, one of her early articles, "Applesauce for All," was published in *This Week* magazine.

Jo grew up in the Red River Valley of Minnesota, received her BA from St. Olaf College and her MA from the University of Iowa, and did graduate work in English and journalism at the Universities of Washington, Wisconsin and New Mexico.

Before joining the staff of the University of Minnesota, she taught English and journalism in high schools and colleges in New Mexico, Utah, Texas and Minnesota.

For many years, she was extension communications specialist at the University of Minnesota, where she taught communications, wrote articles on home economics, horticulture and 4-H, and conducted a radio interview show.

Professor Nelson was named to honorary membership in the Minnesota Home Economics Association, and has also served as Minnesota branch president of the National League of American Pen Women.

Long enamored of the Southwest, she spends her winters in Mesa, Arizona, returning to summer in Minnesota.

More Cook Books by Golden West Publishers

SALSA LOVERS COOK BOOK

More than 180 taste-tempting recipes for salsas that will make every meal a special event! Salsas for salads, appetizers, main dishes and desserts! Put some salsa in your life! By Susan Bollin.

5 1/2 x 8 1/2—128 pages . . . $5.95

BEST BARBECUE RECIPES

A collection of more than 200 taste-tempting recipes. • Sauces • Rubs • Marinades • Mops • Ribs • Wild Game • Fish and Seafood • Pit barbecue and more! By Mildred Fischer.

5 1/2 x 8 1/2—144 pages . . . $5.95

CHILI-LOVERS COOK BOOK

Chili cookoff prize-winning recipes and regional favorites! The best of chili cookery, from mild to fiery, with and without beans. Plus a variety of taste-tempting foods made with chile peppers. 200,000 copies in print! By Al and Mildred Fischer.

5 1/2 x 8 1/2—128 pages . . . $5.95

RECIPES FOR A HEALTHY LIFESTYLE

Recipes for maintaining your health! Appetizing low-cholesterol, low-fat, low-sodium, low-sugar recipes by nutritionist Virginia Defendorf. Includes nutritional analysis for each recipe!

5 1/2 x 8 1/2—128 pages . . . $6.95

WHOLLY FRIJOLES!
The Whole Bean Cook Book

Features a wide variety of recipes for salads, main dishes, side dishes and desserts with an emphasis on Southwestern style. Pinto, kidney, garbanzo, black, red and navy beans, you'll find recipes for these and many more! Includes cooking tips and fascinating bean trivia! By Shayne Fischer.

5 1/2 x 8 1/2—112 pages . . . $6.95

ORDER BLANK

GOLDEN WEST PUBLISHERS

☼ 4113 N. Longview Ave. • Phoenix, AZ 85014

www.goldenwestpublishers.com • **1-800-658-5830** • FAX 602-279-6901

Qty	Title	Price	Amount
	Apple Lovers Cook Book	**6.95**	
	Bean Lovers Cook Book	**6.95**	
	Best Barbecue Recipes	**5.95**	
	Chili-Lovers Cook Book	**5.95**	
	Chip and Dip Cook Book	**5.95**	
	Citrus Lovers Cook Book	**6.95**	
	Date Recipes	**6.95**	
	Easy Recipes for Wild Game & Fish	**6.95**	
	Joy of Muffins	**5.95**	
	Low Fat Mexican Recipes	**6.95**	
	Pecan Lovers Cook Book	**6.95**	
	Pumpkin Lovers Cook Book	**6.95**	
	Quick-Bread Cook Book	**6.95**	
	Quick-n-Easy Mexican Recipes	**5.95**	
	Recipes for a Healthy Lifestyle	**6.95**	
	Salsa Lovers Cook Book	**5.95**	
	Tortilla Lovers Cook Book	**6.95**	
	Veggie Lovers Cook Book	**6.95**	
	Vegi-Mex Vegetarian Mexican Recipes	**6.95**	
	Wholly Frijoles The Whole Bean Cook Book	**6.95**	
Shipping & Handling Add ➠	U.S. & Canada Other countries	$3.00 $5.00	

☐ My Check or Money Order Enclosed $

☐ MasterCard ☐ VISA ($20 credit card minimum)

_____

(Payable in U.S. funds)

Acct. No.   Exp. Date

Signature

Name   Telephone

Address

City/State/Zip   **Call for a FREE catalog of all our titles**   Apple Lovers
8/00

This order blank may be photo-copied.